Praise j

The Book I Always Promised

"An inspiring read that beautifully interweaves experiences of resilience, humor, love, loss, and family ties—in short, life."

—R. Lynn Barnett
Author of *My Mother Has Alzheimer's and My Dog Has Tapeworms: A Caregiver's Tale*

"Barbara Gomes Serafino's beautifully written story begins with a promise to her grandmother—that someday she will write a book about the family's remarkable history. While studying the letters of her ancestors and Ellis Island documents, she discovers the love, tragedy, and sacrifices her family endured to start a new life in America. While she, a young woman in the 1960s, works tirelessly to not be limited to 'female opportunities' by earning a scholarship to Brooklyn College, NYU graduate school, and admission to the prominent Brooklyn Law School, then serving as an Assistant District Attorney in Kings County, and later, cofounding the first all-female law firm on Staten Island, The Book I Always Promised *is the perfect balance of heartbreak and humor."*

—Amy Lyle
Award-winning humorist and author of
The Amy Binegar-Kimmes-Lyle Book of Failures and
We're All A Mess, It's OK

"This story exhibits a closeness of an immediate family and an extended family that is remarkable and such a blessing. Not many families can say the same about the depth of their connections. Importantly for me was the obvious love between the author's parents and their children and how important that bond was in Ms. Gomes Serafino's life and how she lived it . . . Her determination after college, graduate school, and law school is an example to the youth around her that anything is possible if you really work at it . . ."

—Charles A. Kuffner Jr.
Retired New York State Supreme Court Justice

The Book I Always Promised

The Book
I Always
Promised

Family Curses, Stregas & Adventures
from Italy, Portugal & Brooklyn

———

BARBARA GOMES SERAFINO

BOOKLOGIX

Alpharetta, GA

ISBN: 978-1-6653-0565-5 - Paperback
eISBN: 978-1-6653-0566-2 - eBook

Library of Congress Control Number: 2023908038

∞This paper meets the requirements of ANSI/NISO Z39.48-1992
(Permanence of Paper)

053123

For Nana

Christina LeFosse Longobucco and Gennaro LeFosse
1977, Brooklyn, New York

Introduction

T hinking back, when I was just a young girl, I promised my grandmother Christina that I would write the story of our family.

Over and over again, I would beg her, "Nana, tell me the story about coming to America and what happened on Ellis Island. Tell me about growing up in Italy."

She always asked why I wanted to hear all that again. "Why, are you gonna write a book?" And so, in order to encourage more storytelling, I promised that someday I would do that for her.

This is that story.

I always loved to write as a young girl. First, it was "My Daily Diary," those inexpensive, little, pink diaries that one bought at the five-and-dime store. Then it was school essays with the hope of winning a prize. The nuns dangled a new pencil case or a night free of homework in front of our eyes. Eventually, it was letters. Not emails, not texts, but good old-fashioned handwritten letters.

Do you remember having a pen pal when you were a kid? I do. I found her in some popular teen magazine. She was an adolescent girl like me, only she lived in England, and she was someone to pour my heart out to. I remember using onionskin paper and buying airmail stamps and waiting anxiously to see if she would respond to me. When she did, I ran up to my room and nervously tore open her letter, reading as fast as I could and then reading it again. It seemed, somehow, I had found a kindred spirit, and our correspondence continued for some time until we grew up and our real lives actually became more exciting than sharing our adolescent dreams and desires in writing.

I also had a friend on the Brooklyn block where I grew up who liked to write, and we exchanged many letters over the years, secretly written during boring school classes or while holding a flashlight under the bedcovers when the house was dark and the rest of the family slept. We were about eleven or twelve at the time. We even hid our letters for each other in secret hiding places outside each other's houses and called each other "Big Sis" and "Lil Sis." It was funny that we found it so much easier to confide in each other through letter writing, rather than face to face. Sometimes it's so much easier to write the thoughts you dare to dream than to speak them. Most of our letters were about our longings and disappointments, and especially about our heartbreaking crushes.

As young girls, some things were just too frightening and intimidating to verbalize, but never too much for our secret correspondence. Regretfully, I discovered many years later that the fear and worry she had about her very own brother, the "weird" kid on the block, were for good reason. He was the only suspect when various girls' underwear went missing from clotheslines on our block. Back then, I tried as much as possible to protect her from him, to be her "watchdog," so to speak. For a young girl, I had become pretty good at acting tough around him. She found her older brother sneaking around her room and secretly peeking in on her while she tried to sleep. I had no idea as a young girl what she was worried about, but I had a gut feeling something bad was going on.

Then I had a bright idea. *"Send me flashlight signals from your bedroom* [which faced mine across the street] *and let me know if you're okay at night."* We struggled to learn Morse code using our flashlights. It turned out he caught on to our late-night communications, and this stopped his snooping, at least for the time being. Finally, I convinced her in my letters to talk to her mother about her fears. I was dumbfounded to find out her mother didn't believe her and punished her for making up stories and, instead, made them switch bedrooms so that now my friend's room was next to her parents' room and his room was across the street from mine! Unfortunately, when eventually they left Brooklyn for the suburbs, my "bodyguard" assistance was no longer possible, and I learned many years later of the unspeakable consequences.

It was through letters that I learned so much about myself and my family and how we came to be the family that we are. A letter from my Italian great-grandmother to my grandmother, a love letter from my father to my mother, a letter of introduction for me from my grandmother to her family in Italy, and a letter from my Portuguese great-aunt to my father all led me on the lifetime adventure of which I now write.

Since my parents' deaths and, eventually, the untimely death of my younger brother, I have wracked my brain as to how everything could have gone so wrong. I have finally concluded that our family must have been cursed, brought on by the misdeeds of one of our ancestors. Even though I am the product of two rather religious Catholic families, one of Italian and the other of Portuguese descent, we have our share of superstitions. With good cause, I might add.

Sometimes, it's the simple stuff, like speaking too soon about something going well and causing a jinx. Or occasionally someone is the victim of the "evil eye," called *malocchio*, brought on by an adversary or competitor who has it in for you big time. My aunt Jennie was always a champ at spotting someone whom she just knew was after one of us, and she took the prize at shooting the evil eye back at the sender before they even knew what hit them. As a matter of fact, she drove me crazy about this kind of thing when I was a kid, and even when she was at the ripe old age of eighty, she still did. Once when I told her one of the old ladies down the block was asking for her and wanted to know how she was feeling, Aunt Jennie moaned, "Oh my God, that one has it in for me, there she goes 'overlooking' me again," and then instinctively, she aimed her two-fingered hand signal of the "horns" down the street in the direction of the unsuspecting woman's house. Send that jinx right back!

Even at a young age, I realized that when you are dealing with someone who really and truly thinks they are the victim of a curse or some evil spell, you should not try to talk them out of it or try to reason with them. Your best bet is to humor them, even if you have to go along until the thing runs its course. In the end, you may find that you are a believer, as I am right now.

As a child, I was introduced to an assorted collection of lucky talismans to fight off a jinx or a curse, such as the "red horn" or *il corno* worn by many Italian Americans on a gold chain or a snippet of blood-red ribbon pinned onto a crib or pillowcase. Aunt Jennie must have had at least three of those horns on her key chain alone. I remember my mother always had an enormous red horn hanging in her bedroom closet tucked away near her 1950s Persian lamb coat, the only expensive piece of clothing she ever owned—the coat that only came out on very special occasions, like weddings, and more often than not, for funerals. That is why the damn coat is still hanging in perfect condition but only now in my sister's closet even though my poor mother has been gone for so many years! Thinking back to when my mother was at her worst with her agoraphobia, it took either a wedding or a funeral to finally get her out of the house for even just a couple of hours. This thing my mother had about not using or wearing the really good stuff unless, of course, the Pope was coming to dinner or her in-laws were joining us also made me nuts! Her mother did it too!

I remember going through my mother's belongings after she passed away, finding too many beautiful and brand-new pajamas, nightgowns, sweaters, tablecloths, or dishes that were just too good for her to actually use!

"Mom, where's that new robe we bought you?"

"I'm saving it in case I have to go to the hospital. What are you, crazy?"

"And what about the new glasses we bought for the dining room?"

"That's for when one of you gets married and I have to entertain your in-laws!" (Mind you, the three of us were still kids!)

Ironically, when I was packing up my parents' house and thought I broke one of those beautiful but unused dishes, I told my mom, "Thank goodness I caught the plate just in time, Mom. It didn't break!" She looked up at me from her sick bed as she was suffering from terminal cancer and said to me in that so dry and matter-of-fact tone of voice of hers, "Barbara, you should know better than to worry about something like a plate. It's just a thing!" I knew right then she wanted me to realize something that she herself felt she learned too late.

Getting back to those good-luck charms, I remember asking Mommy about the red ribbon pinned to the embroidered lace pillowcase bearing my brother's name in his baby carriage. Her simple answer was that it represented the precious blood of Jesus, to protect the baby from any danger. After all, he almost died in the hospital with the cord wrapped around his neck during the delivery. "Your brother was a blue baby," she told me. She also always reminded me that she didn't know she was pregnant with my brother when she and Dad rode the parachute ride in Coney Island together, and that was what probably made him so crazy. Whatever it was, I know my brother would agree with me that Mommy should have dressed him in red from head to toe, to protect him from all that bad luck that haunted him the rest of his life.

I learned of other remedies against the evil that befell us in our lives, like sprinkling holy water to ward off evil spirits. You could sprinkle it on a person or in a room, and I remember Mommy sending me to church with a small empty medicine bottle on many occasions to fill up with holy water. There was a small gold sink and spigot tucked away in my Brooklyn neighborhood's Catholic church where anyone could have all the holy water their little heart desired and—get this—for free! As a lifelong Catholic, this was the only freebie I have ever heard of when it comes to my church.

If, however, things become more serious, one has no choice but to seek the aid of a witch, or *strega*, in order to turn things around. Italians believe in *stregas*, but nowadays, they are hard to find. In the old days, if you didn't know a *strega*, your mother, aunt, or grandmother probably did. My Italian grandmother, whom we all called Nana, mentioned them on a few special occasions over the years that I can remember, but it was always in extremely hushed and secretive tones. This is the kind of thing that made me realize that Italians would be great in the CIA or any espionage organization if they really wanted in on it. Oh, I know we love to talk, and often loudly, but we invented the "secret" and the Mafia's "vow of silence," or *Omerta*, remember? We also, I think, invented the art of talking in code.

A simple approach, for the truly skilled among us, is to answer every question with a question so that you can never actually be accused of divulging anything, and yet you never look stupid for not having an answer. It is the art of having an answer for everything (which my mother accused me of my whole life) without ever really giving up anything.

For example, "Barbara, where were you last night, young lady?"

"Ma, what do you mean?"

"Your father said you didn't get home until after midnight!"

"After midnight? What was Daddy doing up so late? Didn't he have to go to work today?" You get the idea.

Getting back to the *strega*, the first time I overheard my grandmother and aunts talking about a *strega*, as soon as they realized that I was listening, they tried to distract me and changed the subject right away. They started talking about that "thing" that needed to be "taken care of." Did that stop me? No.

I was in second grade in Catholic school, and when Sister

Columba asked who would like to share with the class their family Christmas tradition, I raised my hand and blabbed about *La Befana*, a good witch who brings goodies to little children in Italy in celebration of the Feast of the Epiphany. When I told my mother what I shared with the class, she reminded me once again about what a propensity I had to open my big mouth about everything and that some topics we talked about at home, like witches, were better left at home. Immediately, she demanded to know if I also shared with the class the fact that the blind baker's wife on Eleventh Avenue was a witch. Yes, that's right, I said *blind* baker.

There was a little bakery in our old Brooklyn neighborhood that was owned by a baker and his wife. He was a big burly man with big broad shoulders, a bald head, and very white, white skin. I never saw him wear anything else besides a white T-shirt, white pants, a big white apron around his waist that he tied in the front, and occasionally a small white brimless hat. And yes, he was blind. His eyes were always closed, and he was usually sitting on an old-fashioned cane-backed chair near the back of the bakery next to the glass and mirrored display cabinets while his wife arranged the pastries and quietly dealt with the customers.

The baker's wife was known to everyone in the neighborhood to be a witch. She was very petite and dressed completely in black, from her black blouse and black skirt and black stockings to her black lace-up little boots. She wore her black hair in a little bun at the back of her neck and the gray in her hair was like a halo around her solemn face. I remember she had a big gold tooth that was hardly seen except on the rare occasion that she would smile. I heard my mother and aunts on many occasions refer to her as the Eleventh Avenue *strega*.

Not really afraid of shopping for my mother in that bakery, especially because I loved their *pizza de grain* pies, I never went into their old-fashioned store with the small, hexagonal, black-and-white-tiled floor alone, even if it meant dragging one of my least favorite neighborhood friends with me.

Well luckily, it had not occurred to me to tell that story, so I escaped my mother's anger with just a speech from her about keeping my big mouth shut. I didn't understand it, and certainly, I never intended to divulge secrets, but somehow with me, they just wouldn't stay locked up.

Somehow, I didn't get the memo on how to keep a secret. Yes, I always had an answer for everything but not the one my mom wanted to hear. Some would say that is probably why this story is being told, and to some extent, they would be right.

We all also believed that our dreams were signs sent to us, and we spent a lot of time analyzing and agonizing over them. I would hear my mother on the telephone with Nana, "Ma, do you know who I dreamed about last night? *Zio* Gennaro! And we were all going to his funeral! What do you think it means?" That is when I first found out that Italians believe that whatever you dream, it means the opposite. So apparently, everything was going to be okay because my mother's dream was a portent, that *Zio* (Uncle) Gennaro was going to live a nice, long life, which, thank God, he did!

So, getting back to the death of my parents and brother, why didn't any of this arsenal of talismans and fortune-telling dreams help us at the time in our lives when we really needed it? And if we were all so busy dreaming, why didn't any one of us dream that all-revealing dream that would have enlightened us or forced us to consult a *strega* for mystical help? Most of all, why didn't one of us wake up and realize that something had gone terribly wrong and take charge of the situation before all hell broke loose?

Nana was a quiet woman, a very modest and humble person. She never asked to be the center of attention, at least from what I knew of her as an older woman. She was in her fifties when I was born, living with my two single aunts, Anna and Jennie. The three of them lived in the same two-family house with my parents and me when I was just a baby across the street from Dyker Park. When my father inherited some money from his parents' estate and was finally able to buy us an older one-family, Queen Anne Victorian-style house in Dyker Heights, Brooklyn, in 1955, the three of them lived with us for a while because of the shortage of apartments in Brooklyn during the time of the baby boom. During this time, my grandmother and I became very close, and when Nana and my two aunts eventually moved out to live in a larger second-floor apartment with my aunt Rosie and uncle Pat, I was so lonely for her company and the way she spoiled me to death.

I can remember to this very day, right after Nana moved out, having a childish dispute with my mother. Now let me explain that my mother, Antoinette Victoria Serafina Longobucco Gomes, was a real, no-nonsense kind of mom. She looked tough, spoke to a child in a direct and adult way, and often invoked the aid of the Virgin Mother in Heaven to give her the strength to deal with her disobedient children. And at the same time, I was a cantankerous, stubborn child, who never learned her lesson about not answering back. So as soon as the opportunity arose to challenge what my mom wanted me to do after Nana moved out, I took it!

We were in my bedroom—because with my aunts gone, I was getting out of a crib and getting the bedroom my aunts had shared. My mother told me to do something—what that was I cannot remember, and that doesn't matter. I said, "No!"

To which my mother replied in her serious voice, "What did you say?" giving me the option to back down.

"No," I did not hesitate to reply, "Nana would not make me do that!"

"Oh really?" my mother shot back. "Well then, if that's how you feel, why don't you go live with Nana?"

So as a little girl, for the first time, I had that sick feeling that I should have thought before I had spoken and wanted desperately to take it back! My mother, without blinking an eye, grabbed my little ballet-class suitcase, threw it on the bed, and told me to pack! Of course, I said that I was sorry and started to cry. I mean,

I'm talking I was four years old! "I'm sorry, I'm sorry, please don't make me go!"

Without hesitation, she unzipped the bag, threw in my pajamas, slippers, and rosary beads, then grabbed my little hand and dragged me down the stairs.

"I told you, I don't want to go!" Oh no, the way that came out was just not right. She stuffed me in my little red-plaid hooded jacket and actually pushed my little tushie out the front door and slammed it, locking me outside. My response was, of course, to cry like a baby (which I was) and sit down on the little metal milk box that was on our front stoop right next to our front door and continue to ring the doorbell over and over again as I watched my nonchalant mother, through a little window, light a cigarette and start to fill a big pot full of water for the macaroni. She let me sit out there crying and begging and ringing the doorbell as if I wasn't even there.

This day was the first time I met my little girlfriend across the street, who started calling over, "Little girl! Hey, little girl, what's wrong? Why are you crying?" Her attention, which is really all I wanted, caused me to stop the tears and howling and wonder, who was this coming to my rescue?

Eventually, I suppose once she had simmered down, my mother came back to the front door and sternly asked me if I was sorry, to which I promptly replied, "Yes, yes, I'm soooooorry, Mommy!" She let me in and told me sternly to unpack my bag and put my things away and go and wait for my father to come home. Oh, and yes, she added, "Don't you ever talk to me like that again," which was definitely not the last time my mother would say that to me!

Chapter One

Like many immigrants before them, my mother's family from Calabria, Italy, and my father's from Madeira, Portugal, left their meager homes behind and sailed across the Atlantic Ocean looking for a new home where everyone had a chance to live their dream.

My maternal grandmother, Cristina (Christina) LeFosse, was a sweet, blonde, blue-eyed twenty-one-year-old girl who emigrated from Rossano, Italy, in the southern region of Calabria with her older brother, twenty-eight-year-old Gennaro LeFosse, on December 22, 1920. Gennaro was a smart young man, well-read, and a real example of being self-taught. He had dreamed of making this trip to America as a very young man. His dream had been on hold for a while because of his family obligations and his required stint in the Italian Army. Those years as a *cavaliere* in the Italian Army only fueled the fire of his desire to embark on his journey to the land of opportunity: America!

Gennaro and Christina sailed third class on an old passenger ship, the cheapest possible way, to join their oldest sister, Victoria, and her husband, Frank, who had already settled in Brooklyn, New York. Christina and Gennaro sailed on the *Duca d'Aosta* from Napoli. The ship was built by Cantieri Navale Siciliano, in Palermo in 1908 for the Navigazione Generale

Italiana line. On their particular voyage, there were 1,836 passengers, 80 of which were first class, 16 second class, and 1,740 third class. It was built specifically for Italy-to-New York service and was worked to death, so it was scrapped in 1929.

Vittoria (Victoria) LeFosse Longobucco, age twenty-one, and Francesco (Frank) Longobucco, age thirty-eight, married in Rossano, Italy, and had previously made the trip to New York, arriving on June 10, 1908, aboard the *Montserrat* which had departed from Naples. This had been a long thought-out dream of these humble immigrants. Francesco (Frank) Longobucco, the oldest male of the group, a former resident of Longobucco, Calabria, aged thirty-one, was the first of the family to come to America. He arrived alone in New York City on December 7, 1901, having sailed from Naples aboard the *Neustria*, which had been built for a French line in 1883, for Marseilles-to–New York service. This old ship had even seen service in the Spanish-American War, until it was eventually lost without a trace (thankfully, after safely delivering Uncle Frank) in the North Atlantic in 1909. His younger brother, Dominico (Dominick) Longobucco, at age twenty-four, joined his brother and arrived in New York City on August 16, 1906, having sailed from Napoli aboard the *Konig Albert*, a German ship built in 1899, which was later seized by the Italian government and used as a transport ship for the Italian Navy until it was retired in 1926.

Aunt Victoria, always called *la ZiaZia*, or "the Aunt," was the oldest of the nine LeFosse children, twelve years older than my grandmother, and like a second mother to both Christina and Gennaro. These three siblings, along with the other six who remained in Italy, were raised on a farm in the countryside, but when their father fell ill and died at a young age in 1906, they all went to live with their mother's family in the small city of Rossano. My grandmother was only seven years old when her father, Giovanni LeFosse, died and Gennaro was fourteen. Eventually, their mother, Rosaria Sapia LeFosse, the five daughters, and four sons carved a modest living out of their dressmaking business and their small farming. Gennaro and his brothers learned stonework and masonry, a skill that was passed down to the men of the family.

My grandmother was always known, since she was just a child, as the sweetest, kindest woman that you would ever meet. Her whole body and countenance invited you to wrap your arms around her for a heartfelt hug. The family scrimped and saved, and the plan was for Victoria to join her enterprising fiancé and his brother in New York and then to send for Nana and Gennaro. When Uncle Frank asked my great-grandmother for her oldest daughter's hand in marriage, he had little to offer the family except for his love and devotion, his hard work, and determination.

The pairing of Frank and Victoria must have been the source of much talk in their little town. Frank was a rather large, burly fellow with big ideas and wild plans. Victoria was extremely tall and thin, even willowy. Not only were they physically opposites, Victoria was extremely quiet and reserved. Although she was timid and self-deprecating, Victoria was like a hidden treasure with the strength and energy of a workhorse. As for my own memories of *la ZiaZia*, when we were little, Mommy would take us to visit her almost as often as we visited Nana. We would walk the Brooklyn streets while Mommy held my hand tightly and wheeled my brother Billy's shiny navy-blue chrome carriage ahead of us. We stopped at the bakery to select a loaf of crusty Italian bread, a pound or two of twisted "s" cookies, and anisette biscotti to bring to *la ZiaZia*, who was now in her eighties and a widow for many years.

She sat tall and straight, looking like a queen to me with her hair twisted into a neat dark-gray bun, her simple printed house dress resting on her very thin body, and her knees and ankles always placed tightly together. She wore those heavy black "old lady" laced shoes and bent forward toward us so we could place a gentle kiss on her sallow, wrinkled cheek, just near her pretty pearl earring. She smiled sweetly and with embarrassment because her bashful, crooked smile revealed gold teeth, no long-er in vogue. Then she whispered something sweet to us in Italian and sat back to listen to the conversations of my mother and her own daughters and grandchildren. She thankfully never grabbed my cheek for a pinch as so many old folks used to do. What I mostly remember was that she always had one of two things in her hands. Either silver rosary beads that she fingered as she mumbled her prayers or a paper dinner napkin, which she folded, unfolded, and refolded again and again! She seemed to be, even at that older age, a nervous bundle of energy.

Getting back to the young suitor, according to Uncle Frank's plan, he and his brother Dominick would plant roots in America. He would then return to Calabria to wed his beloved Victoria. Gennaro was thrilled with this idea since he was se-cretly dreaming of his own adventure to America once he completed his stint with the Italian Army, and this would pro-vide him an opportunity to join his sister in America. They speculated that perhaps little Christina would eventually be-come the wife of Frank's brother Dominick. Christina was so naïve and innocent they thought she would have balked and run for the hills if her mother and older brother Gennaro re-vealed the complete plan to her. Moreover, despite the fact that Uncle Frank and my destined-to-be grandfather were raised on a dairy farm and grew up as shepherds, or *montagnard*, the idea of two shepherds making a start in New York City never occurred to any of them as absurd.

Even ninety years later, when I made my own personal pil-grimage to Calabria for the first time and had to ask at the train station for directions to Longobucco, I realized that things had not changed much at all. *"Perche Longobucco, Signora?"* I told the trainmaster that I wanted to see my *paese* and that my grandfa-ther had been born in Longobucco. After a good laugh with his coworker, he responded, *"Solo l'aria fresca et formaggio in Longobucco!"* There's only fresh air and cheese in Longobucco! Some things, I suppose, will never change, and I believe that my grandfather and his brother had the foresight to realize this back in the early 1900s.

And, of course, there was another wrinkle in the families' plans. After the first three young adventurers set sail for New York, the next sister in line, Anna, married in Italy and gave birth to a son, Roberto, in 1917. Unfortunately, poor Anna became ill and died. While the family was still reeling with grief, Christina, with her sweet and loving nature, became the likely candidate to be the substitute mother to baby Roberto. Anna's husband needed to work to support Roberto and, as was often done in those days, the widower relied on his departed wife's family to raise his baby son. Yet, despite the close relationship that grew between my grandmother and little Roberto, it was decided that she would still be the one to depart with Gennaro to carry out the second part of the family's American adventure. Instead, the youngest daughter of the LeFosse clan, Grazia Chiarina, who married in Rossano in 1926, became like a loving mother to Roberto, although she was actually one of his aunts.

Whenever my grandmother spoke about the decision for her to be the daughter to make the voyage, she would shed a tear about never seeing her mother and the rest of the family that remained in Italy again. Her older brother Gennaro, who was so instrumental in implementing Uncle Frank's plan, was unable to depart with the first group, because of his military obligations. The fact that Christina was going to make the voyage with her older beloved brother surely made the adventure possible for her. The experience and education that Gennaro gained during his military service certainly helped the naturally intelligent young man with his own confidence and in his future business dealings in America.

Boldly, I asked my grandmother one day, "Nana, did you want to marry Grandpa? Did you love him?"

Again, she seemed surprised at my embarrassing inquisitiveness and told me that it didn't matter whether she loved him that way but that over time she learned to love him.

Over the years, I had many quiet and personal talks with Nana. Most of the time, they were when she lived with my parents and me while I was still their only child. Sometimes they were when I spent a night or two visiting with her while she lived with two of my mother's sisters, Anna and Jennie. These conversations were usually conducted with me speaking English and her in Italian and, as time wore on, in her broken English. I always managed to wrangle my way into her soft, comfy bed. As part of her nighttime ritual, we said our prayers at her dresser before a little altar in which stood a beautiful statue of the Blessed Mother Mary. She made the sign of the cross for me, holding my little fingers, and allowed me to blow out her devotional candles so I could make a wish but only after I checked to see that the tiny, but rarely used, chamber pot was under the bed, just in case.

When I begged her, my grandmother told me stories about growing up in Italy. One that I recall is that she and her sisters would carry the family's laundry piled high in baskets on their heads and walk down to the stream to pound their clothing on the rocks in the golden sunshine and fresh, clean air. Once, in 1998, when I made a trip as an adult to the seaside town Paola in Calabria, I was taking in the morning air and view from our room's balcony and spotted a few chambermaids carrying the hotel's fresh linens piled in baskets, which they carried, balanced on their heads! Eventually, I actually made a pilgrimage to Nana's seaside city of Rossano and immediately fell in love with what I found. This was when I finally realized that talking about her family and the beautiful city that she left behind forever only made it harder for my grandmother to move on, and I believe this was why she preferred her stories and memories to be so deeply buried inside of her.

She told me that Uncle Frank and Grandpa left their home in Calabria, Italy, having grown up in a little mountainside town from which their family inherited its name: Longobucco. Nana once told me that the French had named the town of

Longobucco, which translates from the French "long, deep hole or valley." Longobucco was an alpine type of town, and so both Frank and Dominick were brought up as shepherds. Nana's own name, LeFosse—"the pit, ditch, trench or hollow" (Italian)—was also derived from the French who once settled in Calabria.

I grew to realize that like all the others before them and all the immigrants to follow, my family wanted to find their future in America. Their sleepy little towns were beautiful and safe, but for these young adventurers, America was their destiny.

Chapter Two

N ana told me that she and Gennaro had carried all their worldly goods in two small trunks onto the steamer that was transporting them across the Atlantic Ocean to America. She would open her hope chest on occasion to show me her two prized possessions from Italy: One was a faded and crumbling picture of the Immaculate Heart of Mary and on the back of it was written, in Italian, a note from her mother, which began, "For my dear daughter, Christina, as a remembrance of your mama Rosaria Sapia." Nana's hands would tremble whenever she read the note from her mother and tears would come to her eyes as she looked upon her mother's handwriting, the mother she would never see again. The other was a beautiful photo of the family who had stayed behind in Italy, also signed on the back by her mother, as a remembrance for her and her sister, Victoria, of the family she was leaving and would never see again.

Bundled in the warmest, very best clothes they owned and that their mama made for them, on a December day in 1920, Gennaro braced his young sister with his arm around her shoulders. As they stood among the crowd of travelers, their faces moist from the misty wind, Gennaro noticed the yellow tint on his sister's face from the rough ocean waves. Christina was glad that her mama had bundled, for her, a couple of lemons to help with seasickness on her ocean voyage.

"Remember, Christina, you must eat and keep up your strength on this trip because we have to pass the medical inspection at Ellis Island," Gennaro warned.

Gennaro was a tall, slim but strong, young man with a thick mane of wavy sandy-brown hair and crystal-clear blue eyes. Although he had dashing good looks, his handsome physical appearance did nothing to bolster his shy and self-effacing personality. He also had a lifelong propensity for blushing and not only did his cheeks turn apple red but so did the tip of his Roman nose. He wore a navy-blue suit of heavy wool cloth and a slightly worn, plain overcoat. He also wore heavy black leather boots and his only decorative piece of clothing was a billowing pale-blue necktie.

Christina, on the other hand, was dressed a little more fashionable, perhaps because she was just a young girl of twenty-one and so fair and beautiful that any clothing seemed like an adornment. Her face was oval shaped and her eyes the most beautiful shade of blue. She wore tiny pearl earrings given to her by her mother as a parting gift and a tiny gold crucifix on a little chain around her neck as a remembrance of her baptism. She was petite, with wavy, long blonde hair piled up on the top of her head in a loose bun so that a few wisps framed her fair face. Her body was slight but well-rounded, and her clothing was in the Victorian style. She wore a blue, wool sailor's suit with a long skirt and jacket that was buttoned under her bosom so that a white linen blouse revealed itself. There was a small fur wrap around her shoulders, and she carried a tiny, ladylike, blue purse. She walked cautiously in high-buttoned black leather boots. She clutched in her hands a simple, large, wide-brimmed, blue wool hat, trimmed with a matching silk ribbon, unable to wear it because the gusty ocean winds kept trying to carry it back home to Calabria.

Gennaro knew staying healthy could be a problem for his little sister on her first trip away from home and under these circumstances. They were both surrounded by crowds of strangers of all ages, packed into cramped quarters with the poorest degree of sanitary conditions. Sure enough, my grandmother told me that she was sick during the entire voyage, unable to hold anything down, not that she didn't try to eat. This is not a problem that Italian people face most of the time. As she was losing weight and running too often to the water closet, even the other matronly passengers offered her advice that she had to keep trying to eat. She told me that one day on their voyage she was sitting with several other women passengers when someone was passing around a bushel of fruit. She was about to refuse the fruit when a very friendly older woman persuaded her to try a piece. The poor thing bit into a banana, a fruit she had never even seen before. The next thing she knew, one of the younger women screamed out, "Look at that silly country girl, she is eating the banana peel and all!"

Poor Nana ran crying to her bunk, where she mostly hid for the next few days. That is, until Gennaro was able to persuade her to accompany him to the deck, since at long last the famous Statue of Liberty was on the horizon. The both of them joined the many other passengers who, one by one, came to see the majestic woman of liberty, shining her brilliant torch in the still-dark morning sky, just at the gate of the Narrows.

Gennaro and Christina stood on what seemed like unending lines attempting to disembark the steamer and were thrilled that all their documentation passed inspection on Ellis Island.

"Christina, now listen to me! You look pathetic and sick. I know you haven't been able to hold down any food for days, but now they are going to separate the men and the women so we can be examined by the American doctors. Do whatever you have to do—pinch your cheeks just before they see you, and give them a beautiful smile. We want to get through this last step so we can join Victoria. She knows that our ship has arrived and promised to meet us here and take us to her home."

Just as Gennaro explained, the two were separated and led off, single file, to be examined, or more accurately, carefully inspected like cattle, as Nana told me. Whether it was from exhaustion, illness, or complete humiliation and embarrassment, Nana only knew one thing: she fainted right in front of the doctors who immediately sent her to be quarantined in the women's infirmary. Gennaro waited on Ellis Island for days for her, unable to get word to Victoria. Finally, he was permitted to visit Christina and smuggled her some food passed along by a friendly porter. He noticed that she was looking much better now, probably because they were on "terra firma." Then, on the next morning, after a two-week confinement, her release was approved and the two were free to disembark.

Of course, by this time, their sister, Victoria, was nowhere to be found. So the two weary travelers, clutching Victoria's crumpled letter, by ferry and subway train, somehow found themselves at Victoria and Frank's tiny apartment in a quiet neighborhood in Bensonhurst, Brooklyn. In disbelief, the shocked Victoria hugged and squeezed the two of them, crying because she thought the worst had happened to them. She went to meet them at the ship at Ellis Island every day for two full weeks. She was only told that Christina had been quarantined. Of course, she feared the worst. It seems that everyone in this family just naturally suspects the worst when plans go awry, and I guess they had their reasons for feeling that way.

Having both arrived in Brooklyn in one piece, the celebrating continued well into the night once their brother-in-law Frank came home from work from one of his two jobs. Word spread up and down their little city block of mostly Italian and Jewish immigrants, and people came by all evening to welcome them. Finally, Victoria pulled Christina out the window and onto the fire escape, which provided them with the only privacy they could find on a chilly Brooklyn night. Victoria was twelve years older than Christina, and from the minute Nana arrived at her home, Victoria was henceforth her second mother.

"Oh, my Christina, I missed you so much! Wait until I tell you all about this place, your new home! I have a job waiting for you, sewing in a factory, and I will really need your help soon because I am expecting a baby!" Christina at this point was completely overwhelmed with emotion and excitement, and it seemed like forever that the two young women embraced on the cold steel staircase until someone pulled them back inside.

Nana said it was on that night that she first met Dominick. He was a tall, thin, blonde-haired, blue-eyed man, almost eighteen years her senior. She watched him politely shake hands with Gennaro and shyly place a gentle kiss on her extended hand, having heard about her difficult passage. She told me that's when she first suspected the others were plotting an arrangement, and that's when Nana fainted for the second time in America.

Chapter Three

T he relatives all shared a two- or three-room apartment in those days, living in an area of mostly three- and four-family brick homes and brownstones. Many of the older immigrants and more established local property owners ran a business on the street level of these buildings, such as grocery and dry goods stores, butcher and barber shops, and bakeries.

By this time, the two brothers, Frank and Dominick, had been working for the railroad. Luckily, there was an established family in the neighborhood with a construction business that wanted to hire Gennaro because of his experience in masonry and brickwork back in Calabria. Christina was going to sew in a sweatshop with Victoria in Manhattan.

Christina and Victoria had a sister, Acarapita, back in Italy who had suffered a terrible accident working as a seamstress when a needle had gotten into her arm, and out of fear, she tried to hide the incident from the boss. Well, the needle went into her bloodstream and the poor woman ended up losing most of her arm. As a result, she was fired and ended up doing piecework sewing at home. Everyone marveled at how well she recuperated from the accident, how she managed to care very well for her husband and baby.

My aunt Anna, Christina and Dominick's second daughter, spoke about her aunt Acarapita often. Like most Italian-American women of their day, Anna became a dressmaker and did most of the family's sewing and alterations throughout her life. Anytime she hemmed a school uniform, prom dress, or even my wedding gown, she made me count the pins and needles so all were accounted for at the end of each fitting. I remember the time Aunt Anna designed an Indian maiden Halloween costume for me, and as I was being fitted, she told me about her aunt Acarapita and why she was always so careful with her pins and needles. Aunt Anna told me, with pins between her teeth, "That woman was a saint! She took care of all the babies at first so the other mothers could work, and she never asked anyone for help. Boy, could she swing a broom!"

That seems to be another trait of the women in my family: not only could they all sew but they prided themselves on being the best and cleanest homemakers around. Even though they had no money and precious little time, their apartments, and later their houses, always had that clean lemon-and-pine scented smell or scent of detergents, brown soap, and even the dreaded ammonia fragrance. Eventually, in later days when they started making more money, things really got carried away. Like when the plastic covering started to appear on anything not moving. My mother once threatened to take my brother to the furniture guy to see if he would cover a little boy in plastic to keep him clean just like the couch.

Though, at first, the men worked mostly for the railroad, Uncle Frank found them all extra work as night watchmen at neighborhood factories. So I guess I was wrong about them not being able to transfer those sheep-tending skills. They also occasionally worked on construction of the New York City subways, particularly doing tile work. Whenever I waited at some of the older New York City subway stations I always took time to notice the beautiful tile artwork on the station walls — some of the mosaics were beautiful enough to be in a church. I hated whenever I saw graffiti on these walls; it seemed like such an insult to the men who toiled so hard to build them.

Aunt Victoria and Uncle Frank eventually had three children: two daughters, Rosaria and Gemma, and a son who died very young of rheumatic fever. Eager to see Dominick and Christina marry and find a place of their own since the two-room apartment was very crowded, the courtship was quickly encouraged. Nana told me that she kept company with Dominick for a short time, with chaperoned walks in Brooklyn parks after everyone attended Sunday mass. On special occasions, they all took the subway to Coney Island and picnicked at the sea. In those days, the precious little bit of leisure time they had was usually spent sitting up on the tarred, flat roofs of the buildings where they rented their apartments or talking on the fire escapes where they lingered on sweltering summer nights.

Soon, Christina and Dominick married at St. Rosalia's, a little Italian-American parish church, on September 25, 1921. She sewed her own wedding gown with help from her sister Victoria, as all their clothing was handmade in those days. They rented a one-room apartment around the corner from Victoria and Frank, and all lived close to a subway station, which provided cheaper rents and, as they preferred to look at it, convenience to transportation and access to work in Manhattan. Their neighborhood subway station was an outdoor train station, not an underground subway or an elevated line. All the local Italian men saw an opportunity to use the forgotten city-owned land surrounding the tracks to garden. Many of the families, including my grandfather Dominick, supplemented their family meals by growing vegetables there. My grandparents Christina and Dominick had five daughters over ten years.

Uncle Gennaro, the youngest of the men and most recent to arrive, married later on. He needed to establish himself in the new country, and he wanted to save money to buy a house. Eventually, he married his young bride, Catherina, and he was able to buy a small four-family brick home in the neighborhood.

He and Catherina had four children, two sons and two daughters, named respectively John, Frank, Clara, and Dolores.

When Nana's first baby was due, the brothers-in-law, Dominick and Gennaro, made a bet as to whether she was having a boy or a girl. The always enterprising Gennaro came up with the idea.

"If your wife, my sister, has a girl like I think she will, I am going to name the baby. If she has a boy as you think she will, then you can name the baby."

This is how my mother's oldest sister received her name. Uncle Gennaro, the avid reader in the family, was reading a Spanish novel and named the baby after the book's heroine, Inez.

Chapter Four

J ust like clockwork, every two years, for the next eight years, following the birth of baby Inez, another baby girl was born to the couple until, as Nana told me, there were too many babies for her and Grandpa to have any time alone. Every one of them was born at home with the help of a midwife since doctors were too expensive. Their daughters were Inez, Anna (named after Nana's sister who had died too young in Italy), Eugenia (named after Dominick's mother and was always called Jennie), Antoinette (named after St. Anthony having been born near the saint's feast day), and baby Rose (after Nana's mother).

Inez was tall, blonde, and blue-eyed, with an extremely independent personality and was born with wonderful artistic abilities. She was so free-spirited that she was even chosen to go to Chicago with Uncle Frank and Aunt Victoria's family to help with their grandchildren when Uncle Frank tried his luck with the railroads out there with his son-in-law, Patsy, and family, all seeking their fortune. Christina and Victoria were heartbroken to be separated, but Uncle Frank, ever the dreamer, figured that the families would eventually reunite in Chicago. He thought that once he and Victoria settled in Chicago, he would then persuade Dominick and Christina to follow. Well, Victoria wrote Nana that the Chicago railroad yards were too dirty for Nana's poor health and worsening asthma, and Uncle Frank soon found that the Chicago bosses were not welcoming Italian immigrants by way of Brooklyn. Eventually, all returned to Brooklyn.

The second daughter, Anna, was tall, slim, and dark, with an athletic body, an interest in her father's tools, and in playing sports with all the boys. She was also the most fanatical cleaner that you ever met and made it her mission to pass her skills onto the younger members of the family. A tomboy by nature, Anna was always great to have around when you needed a cab since she could out-whistle any fellow in the neighborhood.

Jennie, the third daughter, was a curly-haired, Shirley Temple look-alike, who, as a result of many childhood illnesses, always seemed to be favored by Nana.

Antoinette was petite and amber-eyed with jet-black hair, re-sembling a young Elizabeth Taylor. She was, from the start, an excellent student in public school and a true booklover. As the fourth daughter, she always felt lost in the shuffle, and she told me she had a special closeness to my grandfather, whom the girls all called Papa. One of her simple childhood pleasures was to sit on Papa's lap just before bedtime and comb his silvery hair.

Finally, there was baby Rosie, with long, wavy chestnut hair and the sweetest disposition, much like Nana herself.

Poor Dominick never had the son he was hoping for, although Aunt Anna and my mother, Antoinette, prided themselves on being particularly close to him, and Aunt Anna was definitely the tomboy in the family.

Christina was seen throughout the neighborhood going about her business, followed by her five daughters, like little ducklings trailing behind mama duck, each wearing a simple dress that she made for them—each in a different, pretty color. Nana wanted to fit in and be an "Americana" just like all the other immigrants in their neighborhood and did her best to learn to speak English. To this day, when I am cleaning up the kitchen after our stand-ing Sunday-afternoon pasta dinner, I will be drying the pots and pans and eventually get to the *scolo pasta*, which I can never remember is called a colander. In the old days, when we were all together, with all the women cleaning up the kitchen and laughing about life, the story often came up about Nana buying her first *scolo pasta* in Brooklyn at a local grocery store. Looking around the store hoping to find a colander to point out to the buxom proprietress, Nana searched around the store for an embarrassingly long time until she timidly asked, "Please, I wanna buy-a one *scolo pasta*."

Since the owner just stood there with her hands on her hips and a look of confusion on her face, Nana added, "You know, macaroni stay and water go away!"

The Longobucco sisters grew up so poor, living in cramped quarters over the years. The girls slept three and four in a bed, with the new baby always sleeping between the parents. When the Depression hit, things went from bad to worse. Christina became sick with asthma, which usually flared up in the cold New York City winters. To make matters even worse, Dominick had an accident at work on the railroad. He and a coworker somehow were stuck on the tracks in the path of an oncoming train. They were able to lie down between the tracks and avoid being killed, but Dominick's leg was broken. He managed to hide this from the foreman on the day of the accident but when the foreman noticed him limping the next day, he was fired, sent home, and replaced. The poor man was helped at a clinic but limped severely for the rest of his life. The fact that he was so tall and so thin did nothing to disguise the fact that he had such a bad limp, but his five daughters still thought he was a hero, their papa!

In order to keep their apartment, Dominick moved his little family of women to the cheapest, smallest two rooms on the top floor of their walk-up and became the superintendent of their apartment building. As the girls grew up, they all helped Papa with his many janitorial chores, from scrubbing the hallway floors to taking out the trash to shoveling the coal into the furnace and sweeping the ashes. As soon as possible, Christina and the girls took in sewing for after-school "homework," getting paid pennies for their piecework.

Dominick managed to keep food on his table by gardening in the backyard of a friend's local store and selling vegetables to the neighbors whenever possible. Mommy told me that her papa was so shy and quiet that neighbors rarely noticed him, but when his vegetables showed up gratis and unannounced on their doorstep during their darkest times of trouble, his name was blessed by many a neighbor who had something to put on the table for their family's dinner.

My mother often told me stories about how the five sisters shared one doll between them and owned one beat-up pair of roller skates, so she never learned to skate with more than one skate at a time. She told me how she and her sisters would wake up early on Saturday mornings so they could get out into the hallway to wash the floors on their hands and knees before the other children would wake up and come out to play.

"It never failed," she said. "As soon as Anna and I would finish the five flights of stairs and hallways, Stella DeLuca would come prancing out in her dirty shoes just to mess things up and lord it over us."

I remember my mother always became very depressed around the Christmas holidays when I was a child, and she finally explained why that was so: On the one hand, she had fond memories of Thanksgiving spent at Aunt Victoria's house with their cousins and cousins' babies. Cousin Patsy, married to Gemma, would always let the children play with the live turkey he would bring home from the poultry market. This was the only so-called pet these children ever knew. They used the turkey feathers to dress like Indians and run wild with the turkey in the street called Tabor Court. The fun would come to an end when Aunt Victoria would surreptitiously steal the turkey away, and all the children would hear the turkey's last wild shriek as Aunt Victoria wrung its neck. None of the children wanted to eat any turkey that day, preferring pasta instead.

On the other hand, her Christmas memories were full of Nana having bad asthma attacks and the doctor telling them they had to take down their Christmas tree because it was making her breathing difficult. The tree was pretty pathetic anyway, usually the one the street vendor gave away on Christmas Eve. Even their worn-out socks, which they hung on the radiator, were filled with maybe an orange and some nuts but mostly coal.

I think that all the gift-giving and spending just reminded Mommy too much of being so poor as a young girl during the days of the Depression. She always told me that she never liked receiving gifts as a grown-up. It made her feel uncomfortable and, in some way, unworthy. Her memories of being poor and going without money left her feeling second-rate and with no confidence as an adult.

Despite the hard times, as much as possible, the girls made their own fun with the other neighborhood children. They loved the time they lived in the building above the barbershop. Nick, the barber and landlord, allowed them to play in his shop with his children on Sundays, and they had a secret club, with the esteemed officers sitting in the barber chairs. Anna was always the sergeant-at-arms because she was the only one tough enough to manage the barber's unruly son, Frankie. They played in the basement of their building, pretending it was a movie theater, turning out the lights and putting on a show with the other kids.

The sisters all loved the movies and would collect cans and bottles or babysit to earn the pennies needed in those days to spend an entire Saturday at the local movie house. Their favorites were Westerns and love stories, and John Garfield was their idol. They even managed to collect an impressive set of dishes for Nana, items which were given away a piece at a time by the local movie theater manager at the Fortway.

The girls loved school and most of their childhood lives centered around it. The girls all helped Dominick and Christina with their English lessons so they could earn their citizenship. Nana told me she learned to read English by reading newspapers. The sisters all came home from school and sat at the kitchen table doing their homework before the sewing would begin. Somehow, they received an old radio from Uncle Frank and would listen to the great radio shows of that time, like Mayor Fiorello LaGuardia reading the newspaper comic strips to the city's poor children as entertainment.

One of Aunt Victoria's grandsons, Anthony, once told me he loved whenever his mother told him he and his brothers were going to Aunt Christina's for lunch on a school day.

"We loved whenever we were going to eat at Aunt Christina's because she always made the best and most delicious food. Even though they had nothing, she shared whatever it was with us and her girls, and she enjoyed having us with them! I used to tell my mother, 'Ma, how come you never cook as delicious as Aunt Christina? She makes the best tomato-and-egg sandwiches [or ouvo-pomodoro heroes].' And we really had fun whenever the five sisters babysat the four of us. Those girls treated us like we were little princes! Since I was such a roly-poly, they named me Chicheeboo!"

Now, as adults, we realize that even though the family had precious little back then, it was their love and innocence that kept them all going, and that created lifelong memories for all to cling to during the extremely hard times.

Aunt Jennie was always a sickly child but she had more than her share of adventures nevertheless. Nana told me that once, one of her neighbors rushed to get her from their apartment and was ranting on and on in Yiddish while pulling her by the hand down the street. Apparently, when the girls went into Rosie's candy store that afternoon to cash in their soda bottles for pennies, although five sisters went in, only four came out. Little Jennie had fallen asleep in the back of the store and was now locked inside the closed establishment. She was observed crying her eyes out as she stood with her red face up against the storefront window and her little banana curls shaking as she trembled in fear. Eventually, Nana was able to track down the storekeeper but not until all of Borough Park heard about what a bad mother Christina was.

Then there was the time that Nana had to go to the clinic with Anna for one hour, so she left Jennie, who was sick with a cold, and Rosie home. When the two girls heard a deliveryman knocking at the front door of their building and calling out, little Jennie ran to the closed apartment window and, opening it, started screaming for help that someone was trying to kill them. As Christina raced back down the street with her other sick child under her arm, she saw the two little ones screaming and flailing for help from their fifth-floor window with poor Sonny the seltzer and detergent delivery man standing there in a panic. Once again, all the neighboring women were out there, looking at Christina with disgust, as if she were the worst kind of mother under the sun.

All in all, Victoria, Gennaro, and Christina raised their children and grandchildren in Brooklyn in homes full of love if not money, and they often spent holidays, weddings, funerals, and various family events together. Victoria's daughters gave her eight grandchildren, Gennaro's sons and daughters gave him fourteen, and Christina's daughters ten. All living within walking distance of each other, the families remained close.

Following the example of their parents, the children raised their own families to be very close to their cousins. As one of ten of Christina's grandchildren—number four in birth order—I was always close to my cousins, and I am to this day. We were five girls and five boys, and all were lucky to bask in the love of our grandmother. Nana would bounce us on her knee as she sang one of her favorite Italian songs and hug us tightly. If we sat with her obediently watching Lawrence Welk or her favorite Italian movies, she'd surprise us with something special from her pantry. When she visited us, she always had a pack of gum for us hidden in her purse, and if we were very lucky, as on promotion day at school, she'd tuck a folded one-dollar bill in our hand and say, "Don't tell-a you mother!"

We ten cousins grew up like brothers and sisters and shared many rites of passage from childhood to adulthood together, loving every minute of it. Whether it was holidays, parties, family trips, family picnics, or just sleeping over at an aunt's house, the memories linger still. Our aunts and uncles were like second mothers and fathers, always there to help or protect us from our childhood adventures and misadventures, and it's safe to say we wouldn't change it for all the money in the world.

Chapter Five

As time went by and World War II began to rage, the five Longobucco daughters of Christina and Dominick were teenagers when something terrible happened one day in their little apartment, which paled in comparison to anything else that Christina and her daughters had known before. Mommy told me about that cold winter morning many times.

"I had just woken up when Mama, still in her nightgown, came bursting into the tiny room I shared with my four sisters. Rosie and Jennie were tucked in one small bed and Anna and I in another. Inez slept on a small couch. Mama cried out, 'Inez, Anna! Go, run, get the doctor for Papa, quick! He's sick—we need help, now! Jennie, you too, go call for the priest!' She wanted the priest to come give Dominick the last rites but didn't want to frighten her girls even more by uttering those words!

"Anna, the fastest, threw clothes right over her nightgown and was out the door in an instant, running like a wild woman, followed by Inez and Jennie. I ran into Mama and Papa's room as my younger sister Rosie was waking, and I saw the panic on her face. In my parent's room, still dark before sunrise, Mama was trying to revive Papa and asked me to hold him while she tried to reposition his body on their bed. After I climbed up onto their bed, she laid his head on my lap and I held his sweet face in both of my hands. His eyes were slightly closed, and he said nothing but looked at me like he wanted help. All I could think of doing was to gently stroke his silver hair with the comb I picked up from his night table as I had done so many times before. I thought that if I was calm and acted like everything was okay, Papa would be comforted and say something to me. Mama was gently wiping his face and body with a clean cloth that she dipped into a porcelain basin that Rosie brought to her, and she then sat on the floor near the bed in tears.

"Mama repeated over and over, 'Dominick, it's all right, the doctor is coming, stay with us,' in Italian, of course, because even though she sounded relaxed, her fear caused her to resort to her native language. She finally looked at me and whispered impatiently, 'Where's Inez and Jennie? Where's Anna with the doctor?' And just when we heard Anna and the doctor climbing the hallway stairs, Papa looked at me and gently closed his eyes for the last time, dead of a heart attack at sixty-two years old."

That was the day that Nana and her five girls had their hearts broken, no longer to be protected by the strength of Dominick's love, and the day that the little bit of security he provided for them was snatched away. Christina was now an asthma-stricken widow with five young single daughters. She had no money, no property, no job, no man to shield them from the cold, cruel world. Papa died of a heart attack, and Christina and her girls were suddenly living a nightmare.

In those early days of World War II, they were not the only women surviving without husbands or sons; it seemed that, little by little, the only men around were the very young, very sick, or very old. Although the Depression had prepared them for the poverty, it had not prepared them for the sadness over the death of their loving papa or the sorrow to come from the loss of the men they knew who would never come home from the war.

The only saving grace was that even the poor in those days managed to salvage some pennies to pay the insurance man each month for a measly life insurance policy. Italian immigrants were proud and independent and could not live with the fear of having to bury a loved one in a potter's field. Christina was able to bury her beloved Dominick in a Catholic cemetery and purchase a modest headstone for his grave. He would never return to his sunny mountains in Calabria that stretched out, right down to the turquoise Ionian Sea. None of the Italian immigrants returned to their homeland and families in those days, but he would rest peacefully and respectfully under an old oak tree growing in the soil of his real home, his beloved America— the home where he had helped build railroads and subway stations, helped feed a neighborhood, and raised five loving *American* girls with the help and devotion of his sweet Christina.

Soon, Nana asked the older girls to run and get *ZiaZia* and *Zio* Frank and Gennaro because she simply could not handle this emergency all by herself with five distraught daughters. Uncle Frank was brave and took control of the immediate arrangements, but was devastated by the loss of his only brother. He, Uncle Gennaro, and Aunt Victoria stayed by Christina's side throughout the lengthy three-day wake and then funeral, and the rest of the family and neighbors sent over food and took up a meager collection to help Christina bury her beloved. The women and girls in those days dressed in black for funerals from head to toe, complete with black veils, and no sounds of laughter or the radio were heard from their tiny apartment for days, but all the neighbors worried about the sobbing all night that was heard in its place. Italian women took mourning very seriously and even I remember seeing Nana in a black dress whenever she left her home for decades after Grandpa died. At the cemetery, both Jennie and Rosie fainted, and Nana knew that she had to quickly focus on the well-being of her five young girls even though she just wanted to lock herself in her bedroom and hide away from the world.

In the funeral director's car on the way back from St. John's cemetery, Anna had a sudden thought about what they had completely forgotten. Once back home in Brooklyn, she immediately changed out of her mourning clothes and ran down the five flights of stairs to their building's basement. Each tenant was allowed a small bit of storage space in the common area of the basement, which, of course, was not secured. In those days, this was normally not a problem, since their close-knit community was, at that time, usually safe and secure.

In a few minutes, Anna stood in front of her sisters and mother and cried, "How did this happen? I finally snapped out of it and ran downstairs to gather up Papa's tools and railroad gear and it's all gone—his gloves, his hat, his lantern, his boots, and all his tools! Someone took all of Papa's belongings from his cubby in the basement. How could I let this happen? What was I thinking?"

This was not only the first time that something like this happened to the young women, jolting them into the real world, but it also was Anna's initiation into her new role as family protector. For the rest of her life, no matter how much she would allow other people to hurt or take advantage of her, she would never stand by and allow any harm to come to anyone else in her family.

"No, Anna, you must be wrong. Nobody would take Papa's things from us. What are you talking about?" blurted out Nana. They soon found for themselves that Anna was not wrong—everything was truly gone. Nana managed to calm them all down a little by reminding them that Papa had a few tools left upstairs, and there was his comb, watch, rosary beads, and clothes. As each of the girls found something to place under their pillow to hug at bedtime, it seemed that, for the girls and Nana, this was the worst possible crime that could have been committed against them when they were at their lowest point.

Nana knew two things: she would see to it that her younger girls would stay in school and get a high school diploma, and she knew that they were really broke. Not only did this family basically live from "hand to mouth" but the very few precious things that they had owned, like a wedding band and a gold cross on a chain, had all been mailed back to Italy to Nana's own mother when the family, like many others, was being threatened by Mussolini's thugs, who were carrying on a war of terror against their own people, even before the Second World War began. For many Italian immigrants, sending their precious few valuables back to Italy to save the lives of their parents and long-lost siblings was their final break with the old country—a desperate realization that, for them, there could be no going back. They were truly Americans now and their own children would only return to Italy in order to fight the Fascists and the Nazis.

Nana wrote many letters over the years to her family in Italy and so did her brother Gennaro and sister Victoria. I remember seeing those letters written in Italian on onionskin paper with the fancy airmail stamps on them. Often the letters carried sad news of illness, injury, or even death. Occasionally, they spread news of love and happiness to be shared between the family members across the Atlantic Ocean.

Sometimes, I was the lucky grandchild who carried one of those letters from the mailbox on East First Street in Brooklyn up to Nana's apartment, where she sat on her throne near the window with a view of the whole block at a time when walking up and down the stairs was quite difficult for her. I'd gather her eyeglasses and tissues and watch patiently as she read in silence, and I tried to read her mind. *Was this a good letter this time?* It was often impossible for me to tell because, each time, tears rolled down her pink cheeks from her crystal blue eyes. Occasionally, she'd make the sign of the cross or tell me to get her a glass of water.

Tragically, many times letters were written bearing news of a death in the family—what a terrible way to learn your mother died! No one made international phone calls in those days. Come to think of it, any long-distance calls were rare. How terribly sad they all were when Nana read in a letter one day, in 1942, that her own mother, Rosaria Sapia LeFosse, was dead, and poor Nana had never seen her again since the day she left Italy in 1920.

Chapter Six

So, Nana worked again as a seamstress, and she and her girls took in "homework," sewing and beading and embroidering in the two cold, dark rooms at the top of the walk-up apartment building that they called home.

Now, the apartment building where the sad women lived did not have one man, Dominick, as its janitor, but five young energetic women. Every morning before school or work, the girls woke very early to shovel coal for the furnace or shovel snow to clear the front stoop and walkway, drag out the tenants' trash, sweep the front entrance, or mop the hallways. Never did they think of quitting school. Inez, close to completing high school, planned to study art and design. Anna, the much more practical type, had attended Sarah J. Hale girls' high school to learn dressmaking. Jennie—increasingly sickly from their cold, damp surroundings and often absent from school—struggled to keep pace with her general studies. Rosie, the youngest, was still attending high school. One of the five girls who I think was the most affected educationwise by Papa's sudden death was my mother, Antoinette. By this time of her life, everyone except the older relatives and schoolteachers called my mother "Annie," her Americanized name. She would explain that, as a child, she wished she had an easier name to write, like Mary Smith or Jane

Doe, instead of "Antoinette Victoria Longobucco," which was not only longer to write but often misspelled. So, Annie it was.

Mommy told us all our lives just how much she had loved school. We knew she loved to read because she took all of us to the library every week when we were young, and she gladly brought along any of the neighborhood kids that wanted to join us. Reading for her, as a child, was a pleasure, a luxury, an escape. Nana would have to take her books away at bedtime to ensure that she didn't read all night. Through her reading, Annie traveled the world as a young girl and dreamed of a life that was full of adventure, travel, romance, and beauty.

I remember when Mommy took me to the McKinley Public Library before I even started first grade to sign me up for a library card, and she made it feel like an important rite of passage with much more pomp and circumstance than my actual initiation into womanhood. Come to think of it, she even used a book to "tell" me about the facts of life: "Here, honey, read this book. It has all the answers that you are looking for," she said as she handed me a book about human reproduction. This, of course, was also because Annie was the most modest woman ever born!

All her life, she managed to read two or three books a week and cherished every one of them. She actually spoke about books and authors as if they were her personal friends. Nana would often find her as a child hiding while curled up with a book in the cellar, on the fire escape, or up on their building's roof, alone in her own little world of literature. She loved all the English classics and wished she had been born into the family of the Brontë sisters. She loved history, Westerns, and romance— *Gone with the Wind*, *A Tree Grows in Brooklyn*, *The Good Earth*, and any book by Zane Grey.

Every librarian in her neighborhood knew her by name, as she was a fixture in their libraries as a child and adult and she was on each library's waiting list for the newest bestseller. Come to think of it, I recall at her wake that one of her friends, another mother from the block, told me she had met my mother at the library, and that was how they became such good friends, sharing their love of reading.

I am telling you all about Annie's love of reading as a prelude to why she wanted to take an academic course in high school: so that eventually she could (dare she dream it) attend college. Annie aspired to be an English literature teacher and share her love for books with future enthusiasts. This was possibly the only dream she ever dared to dream—that for her day and age, the 1940s, and for her cultural background, was really "thinking outside the box." In those days, little girls born in Brooklyn of poor Italian immigrant parents dreamed of marrying their Prince Charming and raising three or four happy, healthy children— case closed. And sadly, this was the only time in her life that my mother dared to dream of something special that was so beyond the usual expectations, and it could not happen for her. Young Annie hoped to become someone who no one else—sadly not even Nana—could envision for her. My mother, the ultimately unselfish and humble woman with zero confidence, once had a dream, and then reality stepped in and crushed it and so prevented her dream from ever coming to fruition.

Quietly and sadly, she would tell us her story when we were kids and taking too much for granted. "You know, when I was a little girl, I loved school so much and I wanted to learn everything! Just when I was leaving high school, Papa died. I had talked to my guidance counselor after finishing McKinley Junior High School about going to a good high school, Fort Hamilton or New Utrecht High School, and taking a strictly academic course, not a vocational course like all the other girls. I knew if I could manage that, I could eventually go on to City College so that one day I could—God willing—become a teacher!

"Nana said that I had to go to dressmaking school, Sarah J. Hale, in downtown Brooklyn, just like Aunt Anna, because I needed to go to work and make money to support the family. Well, I cried for days, and then I felt guilty about being so selfish. So, obediently, I attended Sarah J. Hale but stubbornly took the dressmaking course in addition to the academic courses required by the city colleges. Then after Papa died, one day after school, Mrs. Jacoby asked me about my college application. Tearfully, I blurted, 'My mother says that now that Papa died, I have to become a dressmaker just like my sister Anna. I have to help support the family.' She said I should ask Nana to come to school after class next week, and she would help me speak to Nana about my potential.

"Of course, Nana came after school, because teachers were special, important people, and no one dared to say no to a request from a teacher. She was a nervous wreck about the meeting. For twenty minutes, Nana, in her good clothes—a black dress and hat and little black purse on her arm—listened patiently to my teacher. Silently and very respectfully, she waited while Mrs. Jacoby praised my scholastic achievement and explained that I had an excellent chance to be accepted into one of the city colleges. When she was finally done, Nana replied with all due respect and deference for Mrs. Jacoby's station and with such sadness in her voice, that, since Papa died, everything had changed: they were very poor, and her daughter must go to work immediately as a dressmaker."

Even my mother was not surprised when her teacher simply replied, "Mrs. Longobucco, I understand, and I am very sorry for your loss."

Annie was so deeply touched to hear Nana explain to the concerned teacher how desperate they were with Papa gone and Nana's asthma getting worse. She knew it took so much effort for her mother to reveal these secrets to a stranger since Nana was so private and so proud and never wanted to give the impression that she was asking for help from anyone. Annie was humiliated because she had put her own mother into this predicament of having to admit their dire circumstances, even more than she was embarrassed about being so poor.

Just like most young people who are still new at being dreamers, she secretly refused to believe that her cause was lost, and that's why Mommy told us she had enrolled in two courses of study at her trade school. She had worked twice as hard and with longer school days than most other girls since she decided to pursue her trade diploma for dressmaking and her academic diploma at the same time.

Even though Annie never had the option of continuing her education at college, she was determined to get that academic diploma no matter what, and she did! For the rest of her life, Mommy would sew for the family when necessary, but she hated it. She taught her children many things, but sewing was never one of them. However, she was the best at helping her own children with their schoolwork and enabled us all to attend college. She continued reading two or more newspapers a day, one or two books a week, and was the whole family's walking-talking encyclopedia. As an adult, whenever I was too busy to watch the news on television, my mother, who also was addicted to talk radio, could update me better than a chief of staff or press secretary. When she attended all of our graduations, I could see that mix of pride and joy with just a slight touch of her own life's disappointment in that beaming, teary-eyed face, and I knew I would be forever indebted to her for all of her self-sacrifices.

Chapter Seven

N ow that Papa was gone, the Longobucco girls worked hard to support themselves and complete their education. As if that were not enough, with World War II in full swing, these young women were also called upon by their beloved country to make a patriotic contribution. As men all around them sacrificed everything to fight the Nazis, so, too, did the young women of their day. Inez, Anna, Jennie, and Annie, all except the youngest, became "Rosie the Riveters."

The oldest two worked for a time at a war plant on Long Island after school and before embarking on their careers. Anna especially excelled at and enjoyed her work for the Defense Department, soldering radio parts for fighter planes headed for Europe and the Pacific. Many times, she would take out the small soldering kit she saved from those days to show me with pride. When these girls graduated from high school, there were no proms and frills. The whole generation transformed into a much more serious, dedicated group.

Anna and Inez, dressed in their blouses and menswear slacks with their long locks piled up on top of their heads and wrapped in a kerchief, were picked up by buses headed from Brooklyn to Long Island to help the cause. The oldest four of them also helped out in a local Brooklyn war-parts factory after school, working with mica for radios used in the war. They would walk home in the early evening and notice how the four of them actually glowed in the dark; they were told this was from the mica particles left on their clothing and bodies. They giggled like silly schoolgirls as they lit up the dark neighborhood streets, and as they neared their apartment building, they picked up the pace to see who could make it home to Nana first, bounding up the five flights of stairs.

Aunt Anna told me she especially threw herself into her war-effort work because her first and only true love, Frank, was drafted and fighting on the European front. Yes, that was the irrepressible little Frankie, the barber's son, who had grown into a brave, handsome, young soldier. Being the nosey young girl that I was, I once asked my extremely self-reliant and private Aunt Anna, while she was helping me one day, why she never married.

We stopped our little Saturday afternoon project, working on my scout sewing badge, when she laid down her needle and thread, and I followed her over to her prized mahogany hope chest, *a cache*. Opening the chest, she lifted out some bolts of prized fabric saved for some special project or other and uncovered a tray filled with what looked like important papers. She carefully lifted out a small bundle of letters written on yellowing onionskin writing paper, tied together with a blue ribbon.

"Many years ago," she explained, "I was madly in love! There was a boy a year or so younger than me that I had always thought of like a brother—Frankie, the barber's son. He was a nuisance to everyone in the neighborhood. Always getting in trouble, always teasing us girls, but for some reason, I somehow managed to keep him under control when we were having fun and playing as kids. I think I was just too dumb to realize he had a huge crush on me. As we all grew up into teenagers, it became more obvious, to everyone else at least, that he was following me around like a lost puppy dog.

"Then when Papa died, my life changed so much that I didn't

even have time for teenage romance or fun. It was always school, work, the war effort, and also taking care of Nana because her asthma was getting worse! We had no proms during the war, no yearbooks—everything was so serious! And then, one night, there he was when I came out of the subway station after work, just waiting for me. He tried to act like our meeting was coincidental, as he was leaving work at the butcher shop, but he started talking and making me laugh, and he ended up walking me home. When we got to my apartment building, he asked if I would be coming home tomorrow at the same time and if he could meet me again. His face turned scarlet and this tall skinny boy with thick, wavy chestnut hair suddenly looked really cute to me!

"So, I tell him sure, I would like that, and for the next few weeks, he met me whenever we could and eventually was brave enough to hold my hand. We even got to the point of a couple of dates—the movies, the park for a stroll—until he hit me with the news that he was drafted, and I felt like I was being hit with a ton of bricks! He confessed that he was so sorry it had taken him so long to approach me, but that he had been in love with me for years and was afraid I would think he was just a kid, just another friend. Surprised by all he said, he pulled me into his arms and kissed me—the best kiss I was ever given in my life!

"Well, to make a long story short, we had a couple of more days together, pledged our love to each other, and he was shipped out before we knew it! These are the letters he sent me when he was in the army in Italy. As often as he could write, he would, and of course, I wrote him a letter every day! We tried not to make too many plans; we knew the uncertainty of the times, but we were young and in love. After a year, it was beginning to look like when he came home, we could actually marry and share a life together, but that was never meant to be. He was killed in battle in Italy—of course, as a hero—trying to save some fellow soldiers. The whole neighborhood came out to pay their respects when his body was returned home to Brooklyn.

"It was hard for me in the beginning. It was just one more sadness in my life . . . Eventually, I felt better, but that was when I lost my one true love."

With that, Aunt Anna pulled the final letter from her packet and handed it to me, saying it was okay for me to read it and read it to her out loud. We barely finished the letter, but after we both had a good cry, hugging each other, my aunt finally said, removing her eyeglasses to wipe her eyes, "Come on, we wasted enough time now, we have to finish your Indian princess costume!"

Chapter Eight

Somehow, the little Longobucco women, like the rest of the country, survived World War II. They always remembered that if they had been born boys by chance, there was the likelihood that one or more of them would have sacrificed their own life for the war, and they would have done so willingly and with honor.

Christina encouraged her daughters to do their all to support the troops but privately thanked God that, as girls, they were spared from the draft.

Upon high school graduation, Inez, the artistic one of the girls, entered a special art/fashion program at Cooper Union College, which prepared her to enter the fashion world, which beckoned on Manhattan's Madison Avenue. She earned her first job in the millinery business, illustrating an industrial publication with all the latest millinery fashions. Her work was exciting, well-paying, and so exotic compared to the parochial world she knew in Brooklyn. It had been Inez, if you recall, that Nana had allowed, with reservation, to accompany her sister Victoria to Chicago for about a year when Uncle Frank and Aunt Victoria tried to expand their horizons with the railroad. That short liberating experience had encouraged and fostered her oldest daughter's already independent nature. Inez earned a great salary for those days but, like most of the attractive young women then, had a short-lived career, instead choosing to marry a handsome, recently immigrated, Italian young man, whose family left Bari, Italy.

Tony was tall and lean, and very "continental" and appealed to Inez's thirst for the exotic. He, too, had an artistic flair and built an interior decorating and upholstering business from nothing. Like her mother and aunts before her, Inez soon gave birth to her first of four children in short succession, and though most of her time was devoted to being a wife and mother, she eventually used that business as a means to display and sell her own many beautiful paintings.

Anna, the talented seamstress in the group, with her dress-making diploma from a respected trade school, found a seamstress job in a fancy, specialty department store in downtown Brooklyn. She was hired by their bridal department where her talent and hard work soon earned her the position of manager of the department. The former tomboy of the group, she had what it took to accomplish her goals, teach others, and manage others with discipline and a tender touch. People respected her for working the hardest of them all, always expecting more from herself than others. Ironically, during her lifetime, she had worked on thousands of bridal gowns, and yet she never was lucky enough to have one of her own. Anna had plenty of suitors, yet she had that sense of duty and obligation to one's family that seems to have gone out of style. She supported Nana until Nana's dying day and, when her sister Jennie's own career was prematurely ended, helped support her younger sister too. The amazing thing about my aunt Anna was that she never complained about anything. She was tired sometimes and maybe not always a barrel of laughs when her life occasionally became too demanding, but she never gave up, she never walked away, and she never said die. She was the cool single aunt who you could always go to with your problems (when you were afraid to fess up to your parents) and be sure to get help and meaningful advice. And boy, could she whistle. You know, fingers in the mouth, Brooklyn style! Just the gal you wanted to be with on a rainy day in NYC and you needed to hail a cab!

Jennie, the third sister, always had that wide-eyed sense of excitement and crazy idea that dreams could come true, even into adulthood. She also was the sickly sister that Nana protected the most. When she was young, Jennie was a rascal and, when she was older, became a bit of a party girl. She probably felt deprived of a lot of the fun that others were able to have as youngsters, and as a young woman, she meant to make up for lost time. She found her niche on Wall Street, working in some of the biggest investment houses. She loved to flirt with all the young, aspiring Wall Street guys and would spend her paychecks on dresses and high heels for the weekend dances. Don't get me wrong, she helped her sister Anna support Nana, but she did it with flair and a little craziness. She was the aunt who kept up with rock 'n' roll, going to the Brooklyn Fox Theater's early rock shows, the one who was always up for a laugh and a party.

Then at about forty, her old illnesses caught up with her again, and Aunt Jennie contracted rubella, which led to rheumatic fever and heart disease. She was no longer able to work and continued to live with Nana and Aunt Anna and took over the role of homemaker for the three. But her quirkiness and silliness somehow survived, becoming dubbed "the funny aunt" by my little brother. She would take all of us nieces and nephews out for a trip to buy milkshakes at the local candy store/luncheonette and, paying forty cents for a blender full of milkshake, ask the counter man for six small glasses for all of us to share. After our treat, as we paraded back home with our bellies full of milkshake and penny pretzel rods, when the B train roared over our heads on the elevated tracks, she would yell out, "Everybody scream!" and of course, we all did!

Our two single aunts, Anna and Jennie, would often take us cousins to Coney Island Beach, packing old bedspreads for us to sit on and delicious *uovo e pomodoro* (tomato and egg) sandwiches on fresh rolls made by Nana for us to feast on, and treated us like their own kids. There were purchases from the hot knish man who traveled the beach with his delicious, if not greasy, bag of goods. There was the occasional group photo taken by a roving photographer as the aunts reapplied their lipstick and struck their best bathing suit poses while Aunt Jennie would shout, "Everyone, say with me—Hollywooooood!" and manage to crack us all up! There was Aunt Anna's favorite treat, the tall, swirling banana custard cone, to be eaten as we boarded the N or B train for our long journey back home.

Jennie never married either and, surprisingly, lived into her eighties with her older sister Anna in a senior-citizen, independent-living apartment building located on Shore Road, Brooklyn. Eventually, as all the sisters and their children began to move from Brooklyn, there was a short time when I became a kind of caretaker, personal assistant, and go-between for my two elderly spinster aunts. With my mom, the first of the Longobucco sisters to pass away, and the two remaining sisters, Inez and Rosie, no longer residing in Brooklyn, I spent many Saturday or Sunday afternoons shopping with my aunts and taking them out for lunch and usually acting as arbiter between them over some silly squabble they would create. At my wit's end, I'd throw my arms up and, gazing to heaven, plead, "Mom, you died and left me with my crazy aunts!" In their embarrassment, they'd make the sign of the cross and stop the bickering!

Trying to do a little estate planning for them, I learned there was only one remaining cemetery plot left in the Longobucco cemetery tomb. I was forced to explain that one could be buried in the usual manner and the other would have to be cremated, then buried. As you can imagine, this did not go over very well! The arguing began. Finally, I pleaded with them, "Look, this is a win-win situation! One of you gets to be buried in a coffin, but the one who must be cremated gets to outlive the other!" They looked at me with some hesitation but decided to give it a rest, at least for the time being.

My dear aunt Jennie took my job as her personal assistant quite seriously. So proud of the fact that I had become an attorney, she never failed to bring to me a million legal questions. I cannot begin to count how many times she would call me in the middle of a busy work week to say, "You know, I received another letter from Ed McMahon today, and don't tell anyone but he and the magazine publishing company are getting ready to send me my million dollars! So as my legal advisor, do you think I should take it in a lump sum or spread it out over time?" To which I would patiently reply, "Aunt Jen, as I told you last month and as your legal advisor, take the lump sum! I think that at seventy-five that's your best option!"

Rosie, the youngest and sweetest sister, was the next (unexpectedly) to marry. Inez brought around her future brother-in-law Pasquale, when she herself was engaged, to meet her younger sisters, particularly Anna (the next oldest sister) as was customary in those days. Everyone was hoping that Pat and Anna would hit it off as they were about the same age. Although they hit it off, it was more like a brother-and-sister thing. And so, it was to everyone's surprise that Pat actually could not take his eyes off the youngest sister, Rose. Uncle Pat would later tell us all how smitten he was by Rosie with her long lavish locks, looking more like a movie star to him than Inez's baby sister. As they say, the heart wants what the heart wants, and Uncle Pat asked Nana for permission to court his beloved Rose when she was a high school senior.

In postwar America, young people were marrying and planning their families, and thus the baby boom! Inez and Tony have their Italian American–style "football wedding." This was a popular type of wedding reception back in those days, where everyone gathered after the solemn nuptial mass at the local neighborhood church or lodge for a toast, hero sandwiches, and wedding cake! The delicious sandwiches of roast beef, capicola, eggplant, and veal parmigiana were made on freshly baked rolls in the shape of small footballs, and Cousin Mario would say to

Cousin Anthony, "Hey, pass me an eggplant hero," which Mario tossed across the table, football style! Never mind the fact that every wedding had its share of old *goomadres* who made sure to stuff a few extra football sandwiches in their purse!

A couple of years after Uncle Tony and Aunt Inez's wedding, and while Aunt Rosie and Uncle Pat were "keeping company," the third and last Longobucco sister to marry, Annie, met her true love.

Chapter Nine

I never grew tired of hearing the story of how my parents met, and my entertaining, storytelling father (you know who I take after) never grew tired of telling it! My father was from a Portuguese family; his father was born on Madeira Island, Portugal, and his mother, also of Portuguese descent from Madeira, was born in New London, Connecticut. Although my father was born in New London, his parents lived, while he was a young boy, in Brooklyn, New York, and for a short while in Lyndhurst, New Jersey.

My dad eventually joined the Marines. He actually tried to enlist at sixteen years old, lying that he was seventeen years old. Luckily, his recruiter caught the overly enthusiastic young man in his lie, and when my dad's mother refused to give her consent, she promised he could join if he waited until he was seventeen years old and a high school graduate. So, William Charles Peter David Gomes became a United States Marine when he was seventeen years old and treasured his service as the best years of his life—once a Marine, always a Marine. "Semper fi," he would say!

Dad missed his Brooklyn friends, and when he was discharged from the Marines, he kept in touch with his old Brooklyn buddies. One particular Thanksgiving Day, in 1950, after his family dinner, my father was getting together with his friends from Brooklyn and went to the home of the Ursino brothers, who just happened to be my mother's first cousins. The Ursino brothers were actually the grandsons of my Nana's sister Victoria, living on Tabor Court. In those days, Brooklyn was a very small world! So, every Thanksgiving, Dad would tell us the story about how he met his sweetheart, Annie.

"Stanley and I managed to break away from our family dinners in Brooklyn and decided to head over to the Ursino house and pick up a couple more boys before heading out for the night looking for girls. So, we get to Johnny's house, and of course, his parents insisted we come in and have a drink for the holiday and say hello to everyone! My buddy Stanley and I went in and found a house full of family—and beautiful girls! I said to Johnny—the quiet, studious one—'Who needs to go out when we have all these beautiful girls right here?'

"So, I started joking around with the Ursino family, the older brothers, Johnny and Frankie, and the two younger ones, Anthony and Joey, all the while my eyes were on these beautiful young ladies. Everyone from the mom to the girls kept asking Stanley and me what would we like to eat, or would we at least want a drink? 'Come on, Bill, have a sandwich, have some pastry, how about a scotch on the rocks or some espresso coffee?' As each of these lovely ladies, who I found out were the cousins of the Ursino brothers, sweetly approached me, asking 'What would you like, Bill?' I kept replying, 'Just a cold glass of water, please!' You see, I was still full from our own Thanksgiving dinner. Funny thing was, I never got the water!

"Finally, I see this beautiful girl, who was washing dishes at this huge sink, turn around with a nice big cold glass of water! She was wearing a pretty little outfit with a frilly apron too and had this gorgeous smile that she flashed right at me! I couldn't take my eyes off her as she came over to me carrying the icy glass. She handed me the glass with a sweet smile and said politely, 'I think this is what you wanted.' Boy oh boy, was she ever right!

"I flashed her my biggest smile and replied, 'Thank you so much, just what I wanted! I'm Bill, and who are you?' 'My name's Antoinette, but everybody calls me Annie.' And with that, and another cute smile, she headed back to washing dishes. I couldn't take my eyes off her! Just then, Stanley and Johnny came over to me, saying, 'Let's go, Bill, Club 802 awaits us!' Of course, I looked at them instead and said, 'Are you kidding me? Why would we leave here and go looking for girls when I just found the one I want right here?' With that, I persuaded Johnny to turn on the record player and put on some music. Within minutes, the boys and I had all the Longobucco sisters up and dancing the cha-cha in their aprons and holiday dresses! I even got the old people on their feet!"

Every Thanksgiving, my dad would tell the story of how he met our mother, and every time he told it, my mother would blush and say things like, "Oh, Bill! Your father loves to exaggerate!" And every time, my brother, sister, and I, and just about anybody else who was sharing Thanksgiving with us, would listen intently and laugh since my dad was such a great storyteller. He loved people and loved to talk, and when he had his hardware business in Brooklyn, they called him the "mayor of New Utrecht Avenue."

"So while everybody's having a good time, including your mother [at which point, he'd give her a wink], and just before I could make a move, the party starts breaking up! I tried to act fast when suddenly the older sister, Inez, says to me, 'Hey, Bill, I'm having a first birthday party for my little girl on the thirtieth. Why don't you, Johnny, and Stanley come too? All my sisters will be there, it'll be fun!' I told her, 'You don't have to ask me twice," and was really excited that I'd soon be seeing Annie again!"

This was the beginning of the love story of Annie and Bill, my parents. They were young and they were beautiful and fell head over heels, madly in love. People always wondered how such different personality types could be so attracted to each other.

There is that old saying that opposites attract, and boy, did my parents attract. My father was always a daring, gregarious man who knew what he wanted and never hesitated to go about getting it. He was the only child of Bella Aguiar and Caesar Carlos Gomes. My father grew up with only a few distant cousins on his mother's side and told us he always longed for a brother or sister.

Bella was the oldest daughter of Adelino and Maria Clara Aguiar, who both came to America from Madeira Island, Portugal, in 1907. Several of Maria Clara's siblings had immigrated to the United States, first to New York and eventually to Connecticut, but none of her husband Adelino's family came here. I never knew my grandfather, "Charlie" as Bella preferred him to be called—"This is America," she would say—and my grandmother Bella passed away when I was two years old, both of them dying so young.

My grandfather Charlie came to the United States on his own, leaving his family on Madeira Island, Portugal, with only a distant cousin coming to settle in New England. However, my father and his two aunts, Mabel and Alice, filled me in with lots of scrumptious stories.

Dad was an only child, and Charlie had left his family in Madeira when he came to America to live his American dream. I learned that Bella's father was a talented carpenter, or cabinet maker as they called them in those days. Adelino was a refined, cultured, and reserved man who fell in love with my great-grandmother Clara, whom we all called "Mama." She was a skilled seamstress and headstrong woman, willing to accompany Adelino on his dream of a lifetime and join some of her brothers and sisters who had already made the journey from Madeira to New England, settling around New London, Connecticut, where many other Portuguese settled.

The Aguiar journey started off, almost immediately, on the wrong foot. Adelino and Maria Clara sailed from their beautiful subtropical and exotic Portuguese island of Madeira to Lisbon, where they would board a transatlantic ship heading to the port of New York. They were awestruck by the beauty of the grand city of Lisbon and, arriving on a Sunday, headed straight away to a Catholic church to attend mass dressed in their meager but pristine travel outfits. They climbed the imposing staircase of the cathedral and, as the story goes, after nodding respectfully to the grim priest standing at the magnificent front doorway leading into the church vestibule, they were abruptly halted by the same priest who held out his arm to stop them.

"Where do you think you are going?" he demanded of the Aguiars.

"Why, Father, we are going to attend Sunday mass of course."

"Oh, not up here you are not! The upper church is reserved for the upper-class members of the church! You can go back down those same stairs and enter the lower church, where mass is held for peasants such as yourselves!"

As legend has it, my great-grandparents were shocked by his rude admonition, with Maria Clara fighting back the tears his biting comment had caused. Adelino was so offended by the priest's instructions that he never ever set foot in a church again! Well, Maria Clara soon dismissed the offensive remarks as that of an ignorant man and remained a devout Catholic the rest of her life. When they eventually arrived on American soil and were able to begin their new life, she naturally assumed her husband would join the local parish with her and attend mass on Sundays as usual. No! Never! Adelino would not forgive the insult that he had been assaulted with and refused, no matter how much his wife pleaded, begged, and threatened.

He rather quickly found employment working as a cabinet maker on the majestic yachts along the New England coastline, primarily for the captain's quarters. He was a talented and enterprising young man and wisely joined the brotherhood of the skilled trades and craftsmen and became a Mason, joining the local Masonic temple in order to secure the right connections to earn a good living for his wife and three daughters, Bella, Alice, and Mabel. And every time Maria Clara would plead with him about saving his soul and returning to their church, or one of their nosey neighbors would inquire about his religious affiliation (all the family knew better than to bring this up), he would say, "I am a devout Mason and attend the Masonic Temple," to his wife's chagrin.

According to Mama and my great-aunts Alice and Mabel, this was probably the origin of one of those family curses that have haunted all of us to this very day!

Chapter Ten

Thanks to the hard work and skilled talents of my paternal great-grandparents, Maria Clara and Adelino, my Portuguese ancestors had a successful life in the quiet, little New England town of New London, Connecticut. Adelino's furniture was in high demand and his wife's creations further adorned his works. He actually designed and built one of the first recliner chairs, and we had it in our home growing up in Brooklyn. It had a side magazine rack attached to it. Unfortunately, like many unsophisticated designers, he never patented his design.

To this day, we have samples of his work. I have the beautiful doll furniture he made for his three daughters, a lovely doll cradle, a little bed, a dining table, and a chest of drawers. I spent hours playing with the doll furniture when I was a little girl in our house in Brooklyn. My sister has an exquisite table that our great-grandfather created to be exactly like the table owned by the president of Portugal in 1920. He saw the table in a newspaper article with the president standing next to it. He admired the table's ornate beauty, its turned legs and parquet top. He told Maria Clara that night, "You don't have to be a king or prime minister or president to own such a magnificent table! You just have to be smart and skilled and make one for yourself!" That luxurious table still stands to this day, about one hundred years old, and inside the table's side drawer is the newspaper clipping that Adelino saved to prove to anyone that an ordinary man could have the same luxuries as that of a famous man if he put his mind to it.

As Mama and Papa (what their daughters called them) settled in the sleepy, coastal town of New London, many more of their family from Madeira joined them. There, our Portuguese relatives thrived along the Atlantic Coast as fishermen and dock owners, shipyard mechanics, and eventually, employees of a Groton company for electric boats.

Mama and Papa, after dedicated scrimping and saving, finally had enough money to purchase a pretty Victorian wood-frame house located on Maple Avenue. To this day, I can picture that sweet, little house with its wraparound porch and rocking chairs, where Mama always sat sewing and her black cat named Pinky sat on another.

My mom and dad had met in Brooklyn, married there, and bought a home in Dyker Heights, Brooklyn, so that my mom could be within walking distance of her mother, my Nana, and the rest of her family. But at least once a year, my father took me and Mom, and eventually my brother and sister too, for a visit to see Mama. I remember the picket fence, a short pathway leading up to the front porch, the wood-paneled hallway, a tiny parlor room with lace curtains, and an inviting kitchen in the back of the house, which displayed all of Mama's handmade towels and tablecloths. As one stepped out the back screen door, you entered a grassy backyard, and behind that ran the railroad tracks.

Mama and Papa had a family of three girls: The oldest was Bella, my father's mother. Her sisters, Alice and Mabel, followed. The girls attended public school and learned all the domestic skills that Mama would teach them. They cooked, baked, and sewed, and they, too, helped their parents improve their English. The Aguiar girls easily blended in with the other poor Portuguese American girls and boys and even the local children of the "American" New England families.

Papa was a well-respected craftsman and distinguished member of the brotherhood of Masons. Mama took in sewing and embroidery work for the wealthier local ladies, and together they managed to do rather well. The three young girls eventually entered the more genteel social circles and Papa was hoping they would make successful matches. Through family connections, as was the norm, Mama and Papa found a handsome, industrious young man who had arrived in Boston to join his Portuguese cousins, also from Madeira Island.

Papa was impressed with Caesar Carlos Gomes. He came from a well-to-do, prominent Portuguese family living in the Monte area of Madeira. Caesar Carlos Gomes was an independent young man who had learned many skills, as his family was well educated and were property owners back in Madeira. Papa was impressed by Caesar's plans to start his own welding and auto-body repair business. Caesar had already been saving to buy his own house.

Caesar was introduced to the oldest daughter, Bella, with her dark, wavy, exotic hair, beautiful dark eyes, and olive-toned skin, as she was beckoned into the parlor by Papa. She was dressed in her lovely, white-satin, flapper-style dress, which was so popular at the time. Bella was a little intimidated by the burly-looking, blond, and blue-eyed young man from Madeira. He flashed Bella a broad, mischievous smile and spoke to her in his gentle Portuguese, still being new to this country.

Bella and her sisters were brought up in many of the ways of the old country and took advantage of the benefits available to them growing up as young ladies in America. Although Adelino would never force one of his daughters into a marriage that she would be unhappy with, the girls knew that Papa only wanted the best for them and that it would be to their benefit to obey his fatherly wishes.

Bella had not been too thrilled about the prospect of marrying a young man from the old country, but like any young girl, her feelings began to change once she met the handsome and kind

Charlie. Yes, she never called him Caesar. She soon proclaimed he would be called Charlie, the Americanized version of Carlos. And so, another relationship of opposites began.

Charlie admired Bella for her beauty, her kindness, and her smarts. She was well educated and accomplished in all the domestic traits. She never made Charlie feel like he was a backward island boy in any way but only offered her help and assistance in a loving and tender manner. Papa gave them a small but lovely wedding, and Mama sewed Bella's exquisite wedding gown. Sisters Alice and Mabel served as bridesmaids.

Chapter Eleven

W   ithin a short time, Bella and Charlie were on their own, renting a small house.

Charlie went into business with his best friend, Mr. Texeira, who also came from the beautiful island of Madeira. Charlie worked like a dog building his business, and Bella managed the books. Time after time the couple would rent a home, fix it up, and quickly find that the landlord wanted the house back for himself. Saving every penny, they finally managed to buy a place of their own.

Shortly thereafter, Bella was pregnant with a boy, my father, William Charles Gomes. The couple could not be happier! Bella's mother and sisters treated little Billy like he was a prince, spoiling him with love and affection. Bella was a very doting mother, letting her son's curly dark hair grow into banana curls because she could not bear to give him his first haircut.

The couple moved to Brooklyn and lived in an Italian neighborhood on a private street called Tabor Court. This is the same block where my mother's aunt Victoria lived in the house with her daughter Gemma, son-in-law Patsy Ursino, and their four sons and one daughter. I will never forget this unusual street in Brooklyn in the older neighborhood of Borough Park. It was a cobblestone street with attached brownstone row houses, and in the middle of the street was a very tall wrought-iron fence that divided the block in half. When I was old enough to realize how unusual this was and that a car could not drive from one end of the block to the other, I asked my mother why this block was the only one with such a fence. She told me it had something to do with warring neighbors and quickly added that I should mind my own business.

My grandfather Charlie had a local business called Reliable Welding on Sixtieth Street in Brooklyn. After my father was born, my grandparents wanted to have more children. Eventually, Bella gave birth to five more babies. Tragically, none of them survived except for very brief lives because Bella suffered from a condition that much was not known about in those days of the 1930s, as her blood type was RH negative.

After my father was born, Bella and Charlie had a baby girl named Beverly, who only survived a couple of months. She continued to become pregnant with the other babies who eventually only made it through several weeks. I was told by my great-aunts when I grew up (and Bella was already gone) that their poor sister was about to lose her mind. She was a young, healthy, and active woman who only wanted to have a big family. Also, she and Charlie had the financial means to do so, but in those days, it was not known in the medical profession that a blood transfusion would have enabled the baby to survive.

As a means to help Bella carry on and try to overcome a very serious depression, the couple decided to move with my teenage father to make a new start in Lyndhurst, New Jersey. My father always told us that he had a hard time adapting to a much more subdued life in the suburbs of New Jersey. Charlie started another auto-body and welding business, and Bella became a leader in a popular young girls' club as a means of fulfilling her maternal instincts and many artistic and domestic talents. She baked, she gardened, she canned, and she continued to keep the books for Charlie's business.

My father, on the other hand, was now the unhappy one, the lonely adolescent. He really missed his little group of Brooklyn roughnecks. When he first went to New Jersey, he told me he would escape to a tree house and read and wish with all his might for a brother or sister to play with. I cannot tell you how many times when my brother and I had arguments as children my father would say, "You should thank God for your brother, for your sister. I would do anything to have one!" As a matter of fact, when my father and mother married and had their first baby, who happened to be me, my father insisted on naming me after his firstborn sister. He would call my grandmother Bella from the hospital and excitedly say, "Mom, Annie had a baby girl, and we named her after my baby sister, Barbara!"

"Oh, that's wonderful news, Bill," my grandmother Bella replied, "but her name was Beverly!" And that's the story of how I was named by mistake in 1953, when back then, once it was on the birth certificate, it stayed on the birth certificate!

My father found it difficult to fit in with the young people in small-town New Jersey. There he was talking and walking around like a Brooklyn toughie at the time, so Bella decided to send him to live with Aunt Mabel and Uncle John for a few months one summer. Hoping that Mabel would introduce him to a nicer, better class of young people, Bella sent him to New London for a couple of months, and Mabel set him up on a few dates, some proms with pretty, young girls from good families, and introduced him to a nice group of young boys. Unfortunately, as I was told by my great-aunt Mabel when I was a teenager, by the end of the summer, all of the tame young girls and boys that she had introduced my father to were now talking and dressing like him, with all the boys wearing white T-shirts with the sleeves rolled up to hold a cigarette pack, tight denim dungarees, leather boots, and all the other mannerisms of a young, hip Brooklyn teenager.

When my father returned to New Jersey to finish his senior

year of high school, he was devastated to find out he would not be able to graduate as planned that year, as there was a problem with converting his academic credits from a New York school to a New Jersey school, and he would have to continue for an extra year! Young Bill would just not have it. So my father, at sixteen years old, secretly went to a local US Marine recruiting head-quarters to enlist, lying about his age. The recruiting sergeant secretly called my grandmother Bella, who quickly showed up at headquarters and ushered her wild, young son back home.

As for Alice and Mabel, poor Alice remained single all her life, having had her heart broken by a young sailor she met at the nearby Naval Academy. Once their dear Papa Adelino died, Alice remained at home on Maple Avenue and cared for their elderly mother. I never found out the details of how my great-aunt Alice's heart was broken, but Aunt Mabel once explained that Alice was very shy and naïve as a young girl and fell in love too hard and too soon with one of the local boys, who ended up leaving her high and dry.

Mabel, on the other hand, was a firecracker, the wild child of the three. She attended nursing school and met a handsome, young, local Irish fellow whose family was from Boston, my great-uncle John. They never had children, as they faced fertility problems, which were virtually impossible to treat in those days. Mabel worked in the local New London hospital for a time but eventually preferred to work as a private duty nurse.

Working for many of the wealthy New London families, Mabel became one of the ladies in those social circles, and she traveled and cruised with her lady friends, and she and John did lots of entertaining. They enjoyed card parties and nights out dancing and, like many couples without children, lived their lives without schedules or routines. John managed a moving business, and he and Mabel had the ability to pick up and leave at the drop of a hat. I remember my father telling me that a few times he was sent from Brooklyn or New Jersey to go back to

New London for the summer. When he was little, he stayed with Mama and Aunt Alice. When he was a teenager, he stayed with Uncle John and Aunt Mabel.

"That's where we had dinner for breakfast and breakfast for dinner and, at a moment's notice, drove all night on a road trip to the beach or for a night out in Boston with nothing but the clothes on our backs!"

*Wedding of
Christina LeFosse and
Dominick Longobucco
September 25, 1921,
Brooklyn, New York*

*Christina LeFosse Longobucco seated with daughters,
from left to right: Jennie, Anna, Inez, Rosie, and Annie
December 31, 1959, Brooklyn, New York*

*Engagement of Antoinette Victoria Longobucco and William Charles Gomes
1951, Brooklyn, New York*

*Barbara, William John, and Christina Gomes
1970, Mystic, Connecticut*

Wedding of Bella Aguiar and Caesar Carlos Gomes
1928, New London, Connecticut.

Adelino Aguiar and Maria Clara Aguiar
1930s, New London, Connecticut

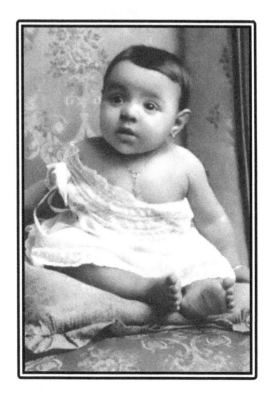

Baptism of Bella Aguiar
1909, New London,
Connecticut

Chapter Twelve

I have always been sad that I have very little personal memory of my Portuguese family. Since my great-aunts and great-grandmother outlived both of my grandparents, I would ask them about Bella and Charlie.

When I was a teenager visiting New London with my dad, I spent some alone time with my great-aunt Alice and would ask her to please tell me what my grandmother Bella was like. She would tell me, "Oh, my sister Bella was such a beautiful woman, and, Barbara, she loved you so much. She was so thrilled to have a baby granddaughter after having lost all of her own babies except for your father. When Charlie died, she was so lonely and sad, and the only thing that cheered her up was the prospect that her son, Bill, had finally met such a good woman, your mother, and that they would be starting a beautiful family of their own." And to my surprise, she dropped this bomb on me and said, "You know, your grandfather Charlie was not the best husband he could be to my dear Bella. After she lost all the babies, he decided to move them to New Jersey and start fresh. Bella had a hard time at that point starting a new life there, and their marriage suffered."

I was about seventeen years old at the time and had never heard any of this from my father. Even though it was the '70s and people spoke more openly about marriage and sex, I was shocked to hear my almost seventy-year-old great-aunt speaking about this. "Bella suspected he was having an affair because he didn't want her anymore. So, she came back home to New London to live with me and Mama, and she brought your daddy who was a young boy at the time. She was heartbroken and felt betrayed. Charlie was furious that she left him and took Billy with her. She refused to believe she was his only true love. Pride stood in the way of them getting back together. After a short time, your grandfather showed up on a Sunday morning with flowers and gifts for all of us and, with tears in his eyes, begged his darling Bella to come home with him. She decided to give him another chance—after all, she had no proof of unfaithfulness, just a feeling that he no longer loved her. They returned as a family to New Jersey, and nothing like that ever happened again. I hated that she had been so hurt."

On the ride back to Brooklyn with my dad, after having been so upset by this news from my great-aunt, I finally got up the courage to tell him what she said and begged him not to tell her that I told him. It was just too upsetting for me to keep to myself. My dad was furious as he said, "Why did she tell you that? She had no right to tell you that! She doesn't know what she's talking about. Don't listen to a silly old woman! My mother and father loved each other, and my aunt never should have spoken to you about that!" I never spoke about any of this again to anyone and never really knew what the truth was. Eventually, I started to think about it and wondered if my grandparents had stopped sleeping together because they worried she would have another pregnancy, which would end in disaster, but that is just speculation on my part. Whatever it was, they somehow worked it out.

My grandfather Charlie died of cancer at fifty-two years old, right after my mom and dad were engaged to marry. He had contracted cancer of the lungs, an occupational hazard of working in the welding and auto-body business. My dad told me that my grandfather was so happy to meet my mother before he passed away and that both he and my grandmother were so pleased that their son had finally met such a nice, sweet girl after he had taunted them with a couple of floozies. That was because my dad, a rebel, always wanted to do his own thing.

When we were teenagers, he would tell us we could never shock or outsmart him because he had been there, done that. He wanted us to confide in him and let him help us because he had been the son of an old-school European father, who believed that you should put the fear of God into your child. At the same time, he would say, "But remember, I am not your friend, I'm your father," with that look and tone that made you know he meant business.

Anyway, when my father brought my mother home to meet his parents, they were thrilled that he had finally met a beautiful young lady from a good family who would make a wonderful wife and mother and loyal partner for life. They saw her as the kind of woman who would tame and help balance their rebellious son. I believe they knew a good wife and family would only bring out the best in their son, and I believe it did.

A short time after my grandfather died, my beautiful and accomplished grandmother Bella died at forty-six years old when I was only about two years old, after suffering terribly from crippling arthritis and uterine cancer. When my parents met that famous Thanksgiving Day, Bella was nursing Charlie, and they were eagerly seeking doctors in New York City that could treat his cancer.

Back in the late '40s and early '50s, a diagnosis of cancer was basically a death sentence. My grandfather had made one last trip to Madeira just before he died and he visited his whole family all around the island. I don't know if he knew at the time that he had such a short time to live. I have an old Gomes family photo album that is crumbling apart, and it is filled with beautiful black-and-white family photos, brimming with lots of happy memories and good times. There are several pages of photos from that last Madeira trip, which I always treasured, as they gave me a glimpse of the exotic, tropical island that both the Gomes and Aguiar families emigrated from. The smile on my grandfather's handsome face in the photos from that trip is priceless.

My grandfather Charlie's funeral was spoken about for years. He was a well-loved man and successful business owner, and people attended the service in large numbers. Bella was heartbroken but strong throughout this ordeal. My father hoped to keep his father's business in Brooklyn, Reliable Welding, open and to work with his godfather, Mr. Texeira, my grandfather's business partner. My father had worked with them since he was a teenager and got his license in welding and training in an autobody school. Bella, on the other hand, had bigger hopes for her son, and she and my grandfather's partner, "Mr. T," decided to sell Reliable Welding, believing that without Charlie there to run the place and bring in the customers, the business would never be the same. Besides, Bella wanted Bill out of the toxic environment of the auto-body shop, which she believed killed her invincible husband.

He had been such a force of nature, so charming and so unbelievably strong—"strong like bull" as they say—never sick a day in his life. Everyone remained in shock as to how quickly this cancer had taken him down! Bella remembered the time they were on a family picnic and she worried that Charlie was too near some poison ivy growing in their vicinity. She nagged him and nagged him to move, so much that in his anger, he grabbed two slices of bread and put some of the greenery between them, taking a bite and saying, "Do you think something like this scares me?" The very gentile, ladylike New England woman had a strong attraction and passion for this very masculine, earthy man from the exotic island of Madeira and was convinced that the sheer power of his will could ward off any danger or illness. And now, he was gone, the man who was thought to be indestructible to everyone who knew him was taken in his prime, and she worried that the rest of them, mere mortals, would never stand a chance.

Chapter Thirteen

B ill and Annie were married about one year after Charlie passed away. They had an intimate and lovely wedding at the new church in their Brooklyn neighborhood, Regina Pacis, which was built because of a promise made by the local monsignor and Italian American parishioners of St. Rosalia's parish. They all promised that the new church would be built if World War II ended and with the safe return of the local soldiers. So they built a new and bigger church for Our Lady Queen of Peace.

My mother wore a gorgeous white-satin wedding gown and a crown of orange blossoms with a puffy veil flowing down, all with the loving care and assistance of my Aunt Anna, who worked in the prestigious bridal department of a specialty department store. My father was attired in a groom's timeless black tuxedo.

Like most young people then, growing up in the shadow of a great world war, having fallen madly in love, Bill and Annie were eager to begin a life of their own and to start a family. After losing his father, Charlie, at such a young age, Bill, who was an only child, was witnessing the steady decline of his own dear mother, Bella, who was beginning to suffer from crippling arthritis. He proposed to Annie just before his father died by asking her to retrieve a tool for him from the glove box of his father's old car after he had conveniently pulled into a lover's lane spot in Brooklyn, claiming he thought he was having car trouble. Upon opening the glove box for him, Annie found a sparkling diamond engagement ring sitting nestled in a black-velvet box surrounded by rose petals. This was the ring that my father had purchased from his own uncle, the family jeweler, Uncle Spinola, whom I remember as a jolly old man with a big, old-fashioned handlebar mustache!

Annie was overcome with excitement and insisted he take her home immediately so he could ask her mother for permission to marry. When they reached Nana's apartment, my mother proceeded to run up the stairs, calling out loudly for her mother. My mother hadn't realized that she had broken out in hives from all the elation.

"Your grandmother came at me wildly with a broom, thinking I had done something very wrong until your mother was able to get between us and explain! She didn't like me much when we were first dating because I wasn't Italian like them. Things were different back then: Italians married Italians!" My father liked to tell this story when Nana was around, especially around their anniversary, and he always followed up by asking my grandmother, "Who's your favorite son-in-law now, Ma?"

Of course, she'd always reply, "Bill, why you wanna ask a silly question like-a that?"

And Dad would always say, "Who loves you, Ma? That's why I always buy a station wagon, so I have a third row of seats just for Anna, Jennie, and you, Ma!" And with that, Nana would usually start to blush and proceed to fix a second serving for him of whatever Italian dish she had cooked for the family that day. Then, wiping her hands on her handmade apron, she'd give him a motherly slap upside his head, and he'd grab her close to him and give her a real big smooch!

Annie and Bill had a small wedding reception at the Brooklyn Hotel Gregory with close family from Brooklyn and New London in attendance. My recently married aunt Rosie and her new husband, my uncle Pat, served as maid of honor and best man.

Occasionally, my mom would tell me about her honeymoon when I was a little girl—of course, only after I would beg her for a story. It was her first trip away from home, except for a quick visit to meet my dad's family in New London. She made it sound so romantic to me even though it was just a modest honeymoon to the nearby Pocono Mountains. She described the elegant peignoir set she bought, her brilliant red wool jacket, and short furry boots, all suitable for a trip to the snowy mountains in February. They did so many exciting things at the resort: a late-night hayride under the stars, bundled under a wool plaid blanket; archery and bowling for her first time; a special cocktail and Delmonico steak; and of course, dancing the foxtrot and lindy before a wonderful little band playing Glenn Miller and Tommy Dorsey music.

Oh, the dancing! When I think about my parents now, I prefer to picture them dancing! Whether newlyweds or when married for forty-plus years, they loved to dance, and everyone in the family loved to watch them on the dance floor. They danced so lightly on their feet and in perfect step to the music. They would glide around the room as my handsome father led and my beautiful mother gracefully followed! They seemed to be transported to another place and time as they gazed lovingly into each other's eyes.

She never spoke to me about experiencing anything else on her honeymoon—if you know what I mean—as my mother was raised in another time and era when good girls didn't talk about "S-E-X." She always spelled the word out, not even wanting to say it out loud. She was an extremely modest woman, and my dad would tease her and say, "Even to this day your mother gets undressed in her closet." But he was mad for her and all her mystery.

When I begged, she would show me the honeymoon corsage she had pressed into her honeymoon photo album and unfold the adorable "Pocono Gardens" keepsake T-shirt Dad had purchased for her in a cute little resort gift shop. If their honeymoon sounds like an old-fashioned 1940–50s black-and-white movie, well, it was, starring two young kids, one looking like Liz Taylor and her husband like the singer Julius La Rosa.

As Bella had sold Charlie's welding and auto-body business, my father found a promising job with an up-and-coming mailing and shipping company as a mechanic. They found a little two-room apartment in the less expensive outskirts of their Boro Park neighborhood and made it their love nest. My father was sent by the company for specialized training on their very modern equipment and machinery for a week in Stamford, Connecticut, a few months after they returned from the Poconos.

One day, when I was a young teen, I was helping Mom clean our house. As the oldest and a girl, I was expected to clean the house with my mom every Saturday from about age seven until I left to marry at twenty-four. There was no going out to play with friends or dates on Saturdays until the chores were done in those days. To help pass the time as we were washing windows during spring cleaning, I, of course, was chatting away and trying to explain my excitement about receiving my first love note from a young man I met at my first job in downtown Brooklyn.

"Did Daddy ever send you a love letter, Mom?"

With a slight bit of blushing, she wiped the sweat from her brow and opened the top drawer of her mahogany chest of drawers. Digging around, near her Poconos T-shirt, I saw her remove a yellowing envelope from the Roger Smith Hotel in Stamford, postmarked May 13, 1952, addressed to her. I guess she felt I was old enough to share this intimate letter that my dad had sent to her when he was sent for training by his company. She placed the letter gently in my hand and said, "Yes, he did. You can read it for yourself."

She had kept the letter for years and was suddenly entrusting it to me! It was just a short note written on the hotel's letterhead. Shocked at the revelation, I sat on the edge of her bed and read, in awe, my mother's love letter, which I found in that same drawer after her death and have saved until this day:

Tuesday, 7:00 p.m.

Hello honey,

    At last, I'm settled down to write. Surprised? How is my one and only girl? Hope you miss me because I miss you very much.

    Last night, I was in bed at nine, read until eleven, and then off to sleep. (Honest)

    We got our checks last night and cashed them early this morning at the railroad station—they have a bank there.

    Tonight, I'm going to the rifle and pistol club, someone is picking me up at eight. I'll probably be home (here at the hotel) early.

    School is starting to get a little harder because now we have to start telling the teachers at the end of the day what we did and use the correct names of the parts we are explaining. Brother, it ain't easy! I know what I'm doing but it's hard for me to explain.

    I hope you're not working too hard, honey. Take it easy, rest up. I'm coming home this weekend, you know! (Don't give me that look.)

    I could only fill up pages with "I love you" because that's about all I have left to say so—

I LOVE YOU

Your loving husband,
Bill

Also found with the yellowing old letter inside its tattered envelope was a tiny, tarnished gold ankle bracelet. On one side of the ankle bracelet plate was inscribed, *"Annie,"* and on the other side, was the date, *"9-2-51."*

I remember my reaction was surprise and astonishment. My mother had a love letter from my father! The insinuation in the content of the letter went right over my head when I first read her letter. Eventually, my dad's message to his Annie became clear to me. Finally, it dawned on me that I, their first child, was born just nine months after my father returned from his big business trip and just a couple of weeks after my parents' first wedding anniversary!

Chapter Fourteen

W hen Annie and Bill were first married, their budget was tight; they rented a two-room walk-up apartment in their old Brooklyn neighborhood near Eleventh Avenue. Since Annie became pregnant only three months after their wedding, Bill decided to take on two jobs. Annie, having a difficult pregnancy, was forced to quit her job in the credit department at a large department store in downtown Brooklyn.

Bella, now widowed, was getting sicker and sicker and living back in New London with her mother and sister Alice. I was told that having a granddaughter was her biggest thrill in a long time and that she wrote us often, sending handmade outfits and items that she sewed or knitted for me. We managed to visit as much as possible in those days, but it was difficult with Dad working two jobs and my grandmother Bella being so sick. We did our best to keep in touch and relied on updates from her sisters Alice and Mabel. Not even two years after my beloved grandfather Charlie had passed away, my darling grandmother Bella was given a cruel diagnosis. Her sister Mabel, the nurse, insisted on taking her to some of the best doctors in Connecticut, and poor Bella was diagnosed not only with severe arthritis but also with uterine cancer. As was done when my grandfather Charlie was diagnosed with lung cancer, the best oncologists of the time were sought. Treatments then were extremely limited and in their infancy in terms of effectiveness. By the time I was two years old, our beloved Bella was gone at forty-six years old.

My father was beside himself with grief. An only child, he had now lost both of his parents, and he was only twenty-four years old himself. Since both of his parents had been given death sentences with their cancer diagnoses, much of their estate had been spent seeking the best medical help available to them in New York City and in New England, especially because one of them was just turning fifty and the other had not even reached that age yet. My father, who was always mature and independent beyond his age and prepared—forever enforced by his Marine training—had no other option but to make the best decisions he could about how to invest his remaining inheritance and to help provide for and protect his little family. He decided we should remain in Brooklyn so that he, my mother, and I would live near Nana and all of our Longobucco family.

At first, when their two-room apartment was not working out, because, as my mother said, the neighborhood was changing and my carriage was stolen from the lobby of our building, "and thank God you weren't in it" (she would often tell me), they found a somewhat larger apartment in a two-family home in Dyker Heights across the street from Dyker Park, which they shared with Nana and my aunts Anna and Jennie. During the baby boom of the early '50s, nice apartments in Brooklyn were hard to come by.

For me as a child, sharing an apartment with my doting grandmother and aunts was heaven, but not so much for all of the adults. My aunt Rosie and uncle Pat and my cousin Donny, who was just three months older than me, to my delight, had moved into an apartment in the two-family home right next door to us.

Now my father saw his inheritance as an opportunity to buy himself a small business in the neighborhood and a small one-family home for us in Dyker Heights, which back in 1955 had not inflated to the astronomical prices of today. First, he found a business he felt suited his background and skills and his entrepreneurial desire to be his own boss. An elderly Italian man was selling a small hardware business located on New Utrecht Avenue in Bensonhurst, Brooklyn. The business had been a neighborhood fixture for quite a while and my father saw the potential for expansion in stock and merchandise and an opportunity to create a home-repair business.

He began a short apprenticeship with Mr. Migliore in addition to his two jobs and saw the demand for a repair business with the hardware customers. He obtained, eventually, a locksmith license and a glazier's license, and with his training and experience, he was easily qualified to repair small household appliances.

Now that he had selected a business, which he cleverly named "Anvil Hardware" (a smart contraction of the names Annie and Bill and incorporating the metaphor of the blacksmith), the hunt for a small one-family house was underway. My father was intent on finding an older fixer-upper house in the same neighborhood as his business, knowing that he would be working six days a week and long hours each day.

He found himself a snazzy-looking 1950s station wagon that would be suitable for making deliveries. To my parents' delight, they found exactly what they were looking for. A one-family, Queen Anne Victorian–style, wood-frame with cedar shingles, white house, built in 1905, complete with a white picket fence. This was 1955 when this type of house in Dyker Heights—with a one-car garage, small front and backyard, full cellar, and tiny attic apartment—was going for about $17,000.

My parents knew the house needed lots of TLC, but they could not overlook the lovely old-fashioned details of a fireplace in the dining room, a stained-glass window in the first-floor hallway, a second fireplace in the attic apartment, and an inviting front porch that had recently been enclosed. It had four bedrooms, and once the tenant in the attic apartment could find another place, there would be plenty of room for their growing family. The house was within walking distance of the beautiful McKinley Park and a thriving Catholic church and grammar school that they hoped their children would attend, Saint Ephrem's.

Although the houses on the block were typically close together, it was a beautiful tree-lined street, and a tiny backyard boasted a huge oak tree and a pretty young Japanese cherry tree. For my mother, who had spent her whole childhood and young adulthood like a gypsy, moving from one tiny apartment to another, this house would always be like a castle: a beautiful home, filled with love and laughter and a never-before-known sense of security. They purchased the home!

And for me, a precocious two-year-old child, the move was even more exciting, because Nana, Aunt Anna, and Aunt Jennie, were unable to find an affordable and nice apartment in the neighborhood and would be moving in with us—at least temporarily—to our new, glorious home. They stayed with us for about two years, probably the happiest years of my little life, where I was the center of attention for a loving grandma, doting aunts, and cautious parents who tried to reign in my wild imagination.

My mother said to my childhood doctor, "Dr. DeFilippo, what can we do? Barbara is eating paper."

"What kind of paper, Mrs. Gomes?"

"Mostly newspapers and magazines!"

To which Dr. DeFilippo replied, "Oh, then, Mrs. Gomes, not to worry. At least she'll be a smart little girl!"

I played in the backyard with our neighboring children, a Norwegian family, as that neighborhood had originally been very Scandinavian. I contracted ringworm from playing in the mud and pretty much hid behind the white picket fence, too afraid at that young age to venture out onto the block. I even invented an imaginary puppy that I called "Bloopy." Again, my mom asked Dr. DeFilippo, "Doctor, should I be worried? Barbara has an imaginary pet dog that she talks to all the time and even named him Bloopy."

"No, Mrs. Gomes, not to worry. She's just lonely."

And why was I lonely, you may ask? Nana and the aunts had moved out, and my mother and father had not yet had another child. My mother, who was also found to be RH negative, had an extremely difficult pregnancy and delivery with me, having delivered me in a dry birth, while her blood pressure skyrocketed. I did not find out until years later that she was advised not to have any more children. Here we go again! Sound like the Gomes family curse? After hesitating and debating and seeking other medical advice, and in an attempt to address my mother's own depression, my parents decided to have another child. I remember as if it were yesterday, while walking home from my third ballet class at the neighborhood Taffy and Terry's dance school, my mom told me, "Barbara, Mommy won't be taking you to ballet classes anymore."

"Oh no Mommy, did I do something wrong?"

"No, honey, Mommy is just going to have a baby!"

I remember the thrill and excitement I felt that day, so happy to be expecting a baby brother or sister—a thrill that I can feel to this day.

Chapter Fifteen

M y baby brother, named William John, was born on a snowy day in March, after another difficult delivery. He was born with the umbilical cord around his neck and had turned blue, what was called, back then, a "blue baby." My mother's blood pressure had again gone sky-high. A priest was called in to administer the baby's last rites. Luckily, this wasn't necessary because the rough-and-tumble, gorgeous baby boy with hazel eyes and blond hair had survived. He had inherited the coloring of our grandparents, not of our parents—when we were children, this led me, as the big sister, to torture him mercilessly, saying, "Billy, you were adopted!"

Truth be told, I fell instantly in love with my new baby brother. After all, I was a five-year-old girl still playing with dolls and very lonely, living in the old house with twelve rooms on Seventy-Third Street. Here he was, a big, beautiful baby boy, and I was anxious to help my mom do anything for the baby.

Unlike me as a baby, born colicky, nicknamed by my parents "the Ricotta Factory," and always cranky, my baby brother was happy and smiling and always loved to eat. However, after the scariness of his birth, my mother, with all of her Italian superstitions, made sure to sprinkle holy water in his room and, as I mentioned earlier, attach a piece of red ribbon to his crib.

As fun-loving and adorable as he was as a baby, this only increased as he grew up. He entertained us with his jokes and magic tricks as a child. He would learn stand-up comedy acts he saw on TV, and after our little sister was born, have her sit on his knee with his hand up the back of her shirt while he cracked jokes and she moved her lips, playing the dummy to his ventriloquist. Everyone wanted to be with him, including his family and the other kids on the block.

As he grew up, he became a bit of a daredevil, always a "real boy" as they used to say. He always looked much older than he was. Being a big boy and in the third grade, unable to fit his long legs under the desk, the nuns had to get him a desk from the upper grades' classroom. All the girls were crazy about him, even when we were kids. Any time I introduced my brother to one of my friends at school or, later, at work, almost without exception, my friend would say, something like, "Oh my goodness, he's so handsome. Is he single?" Yes, he was handsome, lots of fun, and generous to a fault, and he had the best bear hugs around. I don't think he ever realized how much I envied him, as he was always so happy and carefree. And he was brave while I was not.

For most of my early childhood, at least until I was about sixteen, my mother would say I was "like an old lady at eight years old!" I always worried and always planned ahead. As soon as a school assignment was given, I would get to work on it, never waiting till the last minute. During the grammar-school years, while on Christmas and Easter vacations, I would cry and beg my mother to buy me new school note tablets so I could rewrite all my notes. I did this not only so they would be neat but because I thought that in the rewriting, I would reinforce all that grammar-school knowledge into my nervous little head. I never really competed with other kids, and my parents never had to pressure me or supervise my work, I just did it to myself.

My brother, on the other hand, was more naturally smart and it seemed that his school lessons came more easily to him.

According to my mother's *Better Homes and Gardens* baby book, some of the first things I said when I was a baby were, "What are you doing?" "Make sure!" "What's the matter?" and "Why?" So you can see that this was my neurotic personality from the very start.

Even though I may have been a nerd in the classroom and always drove myself to do my best in school—which resulted in my father calling me, "school smart, home stupid"—I also managed to keep my reputation at home for being a blabbermouth. Once, Mommy took Billy and me Christmas shopping on Eighty-Sixth Street in Brooklyn a few days before the big day. We bundled up, and Billy, about three, was wearing a snowsuit, one of those bulky things that made it impossible for a child to walk or bend. We took the Fort Hamilton Parkway bus and got off in front of a five-and-ten-cent store and made very few purchases. There was a quick bite at a luncheonette, my mom's favorite, where we each had a cup of chicken soup and shared a grilled cheese sandwich accompanied by cups of hot cocoa.

Next, we made our way along Eighty-Sixth Street and turned the corner onto Fifth Avenue. There was something for Nana at a women's specialty shop, something for Aunt Anna and Jennie at a fancy candy store, and just as it began to snow heavily, a last stop at a fine men's shop for a gift for my dad.

By the time we were done, the snow was really coming down and it was very cold. Mommy decided we should keep moving, advancing to the next bus stop in the direction of home. Billy was having a hard time walking in his snow suit with his little baby steps. Mommy picked him up and handed some of our bundles to me. By the time we made it all the way to Seventy-Fifth Street, my mother noticed a bus finally heading in our direction. It seemed to take forever for the bus to make it from Third Avenue to Fifth Avenue, and as Billy was crying, she kept rubbing his hands and his chubby cheeks. I will never forget the nervous look on my mother's face because she never did anything risky.

The next thing you know, one of the old ladies waiting at the bus stop with us said, "What kind of a mother takes a baby out in a snowstorm?"

To which my mother replied, "It wasn't snowing when we left the house!"

We finally boarded the bus which carried us a few stops to Eleventh Avenue, enough time for us to warm up a little and regroup. We walked the couple of blocks home after getting off the bus and, once home, stripped down to our underwear to take a nice hot bath. I remember by the time Dad got home from work, we had already eaten dinner and were in our footie pajamas.

As always, we were excited to have him home with us and I would get his slippers while he washed up and prepared to eat. Mom arranged his dinner as he sat in his recliner to relax a minute after a twelve-hour day at work. "Daddy, we went Christmas shopping today and got caught in a blizzard and an old lady told Mommy she was a bad mother!" Then, of course, my mom, who was in the kitchen and annoyed at what she heard, called out, "Barbara, don't say anything about what we did today!"

To which I yelled back, "Don't worry, Mommy, I won't tell Daddy that we bought him black leather gloves for Christmas!"

Chapter Sixteen

Our small close-knit Italian American family began to grow with my aunt Inez and uncle Tony having four children and my aunt Rosie and uncle Pat having three. All of our holidays and birthday celebrations were spent together, always including, most importantly, Nana and Aunts Anna and Jennie, the centerpiece of it all.

We always enjoyed an annual family picnic at a local state park, packing along a feast fit for a king. The uncles would buy fresh donuts and buns from the best Brooklyn bakeries while the aunts brewed the best coffee in percolators on the outdoor grills.

We would run around and play ball or tag with the uncles while Nana and the aunts started to cook the Sunday gravy (oh yes, this was an Italian American picnic) and boiled the water for the pasta in a giant pot. After Sunday dinner, they would lie around and take in the sun, read the Sunday papers in their cute shorts or sundresses, and the men would play cards.

At about six o'clock, the hot dogs and steaks would hit the grill, accompanied by a huge, delicious salad. As the ladies started to clean up, washing the dishes and pots at the old-fashioned water pumps, we cousins roasted marshmallows supervised by the uncles. I have a photo of me at about four years old, with my cute ponytail, roasting a marshmallow on a stick about five feet long! You never know, you just can't get too close to the fire!

One year, while the uncles sat at the picnic table wearing their checkered shirts, black socks, and sandals and smoking away, and while Nana and the aunts were finally relaxing, reading and chatting, three of the younger cousins had climbed into my dad's '69 station wagon and accidentally hit the stick shift, causing the car to roll in reverse down the hill, heading straight for the spot where the littlest baby cousin lay napping on a blanket. My dad, never missing a trick, jumped up from the picnic table, ran to the car, and dove onto the front seat, stopping the disaster from happening! After all the younger cousins had a good cry, the rosary beads came out, and Dad and the uncles went back to their poker game.

While her two married sisters were adding to their families, my mother began praying for another child of her own, even against medical advice. It had been six years since my brother was born, and my mother was feeling sad about her biological clock ticking away. She wanted more children; she missed having babies. She had been told firmly by her doctors, "No more babies," but she apparently hounded my father to try one more time. So, seven years after my brother, a beautiful baby girl named Christina, after Nana, was born to our family. She had been born breech, and yes, my mother's blood pressure had soared again, and she barely escaped a stroke. My baby sister was tiny and pink and born with lots of dark black hair, which stood up straight like a pineapple, as my mom said. Again, I remember the day Mom and Dad brought her home, during another snowstorm.

I was about to have lunch at a neighbor's house when I spotted Dad's station wagon coming down the block.

"Please, Mrs. Rocco, may I be excused? I'm dying to see the new baby!"

She laughed as I pulled on my boots and jacket and ran down the street in the snow drifts, grabbing my mom around the hips and jumping up and down to see the new baby. Billy eventually joined us after finishing his lunch. I then begged my mom if I could sit in a chair next to the crib, which she kept on the first floor in the back room, and watch the baby while she and Dad had lunch.

"Of course," she said. "I'll even let you finish your lunch sitting next to the crib if you promise not to get any crumbs on the floor."

I thought to myself, *This really must be a special occasion. That was never allowed.* I sat next to the crib for hours, staring at that baby girl and falling in love again. I was a twelve-year-old girl who started to believe that Mom brought this baby home just for me.

Christina was Nana's last grandchild, the youngest cousin and the little darling of the entire family to this day. My parents named her perfectly because, just like our grandmother, she was and is the sweetest person you would ever want to meet. Her straight, spiky black hair eventually grew into beautiful black ringlets, and she always had and has pretty pink cheeks. As you will see, and as things worked out, I have always been so grateful that Mom insisted on just one more baby.

Even though I am almost twelve years older than my sister, Christina, we are very close. As the years went by, I could not help but feel like a second mother to her. We are sisters and we are friends and have always been there for each other.

I cannot speak for my sister, but this memory will always be special to me: When I was married at twenty-four years old and moving into an apartment with my husband, my little sister was to move into my larger bedroom. She had a tiny bedroom, which we had always referred to as "the baby room." It didn't even have its own closet. In all these years, I've never met anyone that wasn't excited to move into their older brother's or sister's bedroom if the room was larger.

As my wedding day got closer, I would ask her, "Isn't this exciting, Dee [our nickname for Christina]? You'll be getting a nice big bedroom with your own closet!" She never answered me. Most younger siblings would move into the empty larger bedroom on the wedding *night*! Not my little sister. I found out from my mother that my sister was so sad I had moved out of the house that it took her a whole month to leave her bedroom and sleep in my room.

I'm not saying that my brother and sister and I didn't have our quarrels or differences or that we didn't have the normal amount of sibling rivalry, especially when we were younger, but I believe we have had a truly loving relationship throughout our lives, and we would do anything to help each other and, yes, give anything to be together again.

Chapter Seventeen

I was a typical baby boomer that spent my early childhood in the '50s and '60s at the height of America's prosperity and what I'd call "innocence." Most of those years were spent nourished by the love of my family and surviving the growing pains of childhood with neighborhood friends.

For me, school was all-encompassing. Our parents, like many others in those days, were lucky to have graduated from high school and wanted to have more for their children, and so they scrimped and saved to send us to private Catholic schools. I can always remember wanting to go to college and to "be somebody." I'm not sure if I knew what that really meant.

I know that my father regretted not taking the opportunity offered to him by his parents to go to college. However, neither of my parents ever had to encourage or entice me to go to college. It was what I wanted. My mother's biggest disappointment in life was that she had not been allowed to go to college, that she had been forced to go to an all-girls trade school which she hated. We never heard the end of that!

She never would teach me how to use a sewing machine! "Get a good education and you can hire someone to sew for you," she would say. I only wanted to be somebody or something and to be independent. Most girls in those days wanted to get married and have children. I just never thought that way. I do remember the nuns every year making an effort to encourage religious vocations for girls, and I remember asking one nun, Sister Charles Borromeo, "How do you know when you get 'the call'?" (as it was always referred to), and the answer was always, "You'll know!" I went home and told my mother, "Please, Mom, don't answer the phone, whatever you do!"

During my early school days, we were living with the ramifications of the Cold War. We practiced air-raid drills during grade school with the sirens screaming and the nuns hastening us to hide under our desks or under our jackets in the closets as they walked up and down the hallways saying their rosary beads. I watched Nikita Khrushchev banging his shoe on the desk as he argued with President John F. Kennedy. I lived through many other traumatic events in our American history: The day of the assassination of our beloved and inspiring President Kennedy, Sister Eunice, the principal, announced over the PA that he had been shot and killed. We were stunned, as the nuns cried and ushered us out of our school, to go home and pray for our country. I was in fifth grade. I remember crying and seeing all the adults out on the streets crying. I saw my mother crying over these horrific events on television. We all watched his funeral on television, and it seemed like the whole world had come to a stop and every grown-up I knew was crying. In shock, I was terrified to see on live television that Lee Harvey Oswald was shot and killed by Jack Ruby. These were devastating events that shaped our young lives forever.

When it was time to select a high school, I had but one choice, of course: the one college preparatory high school that there was for girls in Brooklyn. I hadn't even realized that such schools existed until one of my classmates, whose mother was a teacher, informed me so. I begged my parents to let me go even though the school was located in the Park Slope section of Brooklyn, which would require me to take a bus and two subway trains to attend classes in such a faraway neighborhood. They wanted me to stay near home, but after speaking to my friend's mother, they consented.

Although it was a very competitive school, and we were required to take difficult courses and every Regents exam given, I wanted to go. The requirements were tough: two languages and every math and science class that was given in high school. We had a math club, science clubs, language clubs, and the National Honor Society. We were even offered Advanced Placement classes for college credit, which was the first time this had been done in New York City. It was a no-nonsense school. Art and music and other cultural courses were offered but not emphasized. None of the secretarial courses offered in other girls' high schools were taught. It was an all-girls Catholic high school, where we were told that if we worked hard, we could be whatever we wanted to be. This was unusual for girls in those days.

Then in the late '60s and early '70s, the world changed again. The Vietnam War was raging and so were antiwar demonstrations. A few of our younger lay teachers incorporated folk music and more radical literature into our lessons. On a warm, sunny spring day, we would take our French class outside to nearby Prospect Park and sit on blankets and discuss French philosophy, which always led to current events. We had field trips to nearby New York City, to museums and Greenwich Village.

I remember the assassinations of Martin Luther King Jr. and Bobby Kennedy and watching the evening news filled with video of the bloody Vietnam War. Antiwar groups were rioting in the streets, and race riots filled the news. I cried myself to sleep many nights, not knowing how to take this all in as a young teenager.

At sixteen, I marched in my first antiwar demonstration, carrying a large sign with the name of a soldier killed in the Vietnam War. With my cousin Donny, we listened to alternative rock music on FM radio, and we purchased tickets to attend the Woodstock music festival. Most of these things my parents knew nothing about. After doing my Saturday chores, I would sneak away with friends to Greenwich Village or Central Park to attend demonstrations against the war or pro–women's liberation rallies and free rock 'n' roll concerts.

Well, there was that time my dad spotted me marching in a local antiwar demonstration in our own neighborhood, and as I saw his beat-up, old station wagon drive by us, I knew there would be hell to pay. After all, my dad was a US Marine—"was" as in the present, not as in the past. As my dad always said, "Once a Marine, always a Marine! Semper Fi!" He and I had lots of political arguments in those days as my mother and I had lots of arguments about more personal things: what I should wear, how I should look—long hair, no makeup, no bra—how I should behave, you name it. I'm so sorry now about how difficult I was back then. I thought I knew it all, and if they would not give me permission, my strategy became a don't ask, don't tell policy!

There was one big hitch and that was, how do I go to Woodstock in upstate New York for a couple of days without them missing me? Well, I tried every means possible to get their approval. I tried begging, I tried hysteria, I tried threatening all kinds of things, to which my father responded, "Are you crazy? You're only sixteen, and I don't care who you're going with! The answer is no! And if you dare step outside the door this weekend, don't bother trying to get back in because I will change the locks!" *Crap*, I thought, *he really means it*. I knew my father had a locksmith license for the hardware business and that changing the locks for him would be so easy and not cost him a cent.

My devious teenage mind never gave up, and I spent that summer reading every book or newspaper about the counterculture. I decided to start an underground, independent student newspaper. I had a meeting with a few like-minded high school friends and asked for contributions to the paper. We were tired of working on the school newspaper and having to get permission and approval for every article and every cartoon. So I used my father's mimeograph machine at his hardware store and printed off maybe one hundred copies of the paper I called

"Nyanza," after a beautiful sailboat that I saw that summer on a trip to visit our family in New London.

When school started up again, other contributors and I stood on the corner of Sixth Street, giving out our paper to classmates. This went on successfully for a couple of months, as interest among readers grew and many school friends wanted to contribute their poems, news stories, or artwork. It continued at least until the nun who was in charge of the school newspaper caught wind of it and I was personally instructed by my homeroom nun, Sister Clarence Mary, that the principal wanted to see me.

Okay, so this was not the first time I was invited to a meeting with the principal. There was the time I wasn't happy with the new strict French teacher I had been assigned. Seeing that the young, hip French lay teacher I preferred had a class at the same time, I persuaded a close classmate to join me as we just marched into the other class. "No one will notice," I told her. Famous last words! We did this for about a week until one morning, Sister Clarence Mary stood up like a Marine sergeant and, with a red face, yelled at me, "Ms. Gomes, who died and made you principal?" Off I went for a meeting with the real living and breathing principal, Sister Innocenta. Our punishment was to speak to the janitor and tell him not to clean our homeroom for one month, because my friend and I were the new janitors.

There were other meetings with the principal over things like smoking in the cafeteria or being allowed to wear jeans while commuting on the subways instead of our school uniforms. We actually won some of these causes.

But the meeting over my underground newspaper did not go well. I had to immediately stop and desist or else. There was no reason for her to explain what "or else" meant. She sat calmly and spoke very slowly and almost in a whisper, but her reddened face and the veins popping out of her habit said it all. I was angry and felt that my constitutional rights were being violated but, wanting to go to college so much, I gave up. I decided to finish high school on a high note, or at least a quiet one. I set my sights on getting into the most liberal colleges in New York City that I could find and afford. No more uptight nuns and Catholic schools for me! Hell, twelve years was enough.

Chapter Eighteen

I wanted to go away to college, but my father would not have it. "You, young lady, will remain under my roof." I don't want to give you the impression that either my father or my mother were unloving disciplinarians. They were completely loving parents who were always there for us. Everything they did, they did for their children. They sacrificed all of their married life for us. They were proud of us, encouraged us, and helped us. Yet they were no-nonsense parents. My mom was famous for such lines as "Keep crying and I'll give you something to cry about" and "I don't care what the other mothers say." My father gave the three of us a speech early on when we would cry if he said no to something that we asked for: "Let's just get this straight—when you ask me for something, just expect no. This way when I say no, you won't be disappointed and I won't have to be annoyed." This is why one Father's Day, the three of us chipped in and bought him a T-shirt that we special ordered which read in big letters, "EXPECT NO!"

In this case, when he forbade me to go away to college, he did the right thing. I know now that he knew exactly whom he was dealing with and just how much freedom I could handle. Although I was accepted at NYU, my first choice, I received only a partial scholarship, which in those days meant that my parents would have to make a $1,500-a-year "family contribution." My father sat me down and explained that with three children to support, this would not be financially possible. We realized that if I attended Brooklyn College, which in those days had free tuition, then my Regents scholarship would pay for all of my expenses, such as books.

So, to Brooklyn College I went. And I loved it! I loved every minute of those four years even though I was commuting from home. I loved the freedom, the diversity, and the extraordinary experiences that I devoured! There was streaking on campus, there were political demonstrations and rallies, and there was a cultural exposure that I had longed for. After twelve years of Catholic school, I was now in class with all kinds of races, ethnic groups, and very importantly, after four years at an all-girls high school—boys!

You could actually take yoga or fencing as a physical education class. I joined the college radio station and learned to read the news on air that I grabbed hot off the presses from our Associated Press teletype machine. You could hear Jane Fonda and Tom Hayden speak in the quadrangle. Baba Ram Dass and Hare Krishnas were all over the campus ready to engage in philosophical debates. I switched my major from pre-med to philosophy. The once uptight and very practical young girl I had been chose passion over practicality. I read Eastern and Western philosophy books. I read books like *Be Here Now, Our Bodies Ourselves*, and *Steal This Book*. I was in heaven!

The one thing I was missing and longed to experience was getting out of Brooklyn and seeing the world. I wanted to join all the throngs of American college students who were backpacking through Europe at the time. My parents would not hear about studying abroad or the Peace Corps. I would have to settle for something less long term that they would be comfortable with. After brainstorming with a good friend of mine who also was longing to hit the road, we found that there was an employment agency in Manhattan that, for $200, would find you three options for summer jobs in Europe. We were friends from high school and college and kindred spirits in many ways, especially in seeking independence and adventure. This was our hope for the summer of '74, the summer between our junior and senior year at Brooklyn College.

We had saved the money from working after school, and we had carefully selected a country we hoped our parents would approve of. We chose Switzerland. How neutral could you get? We chose Switzerland because my friend's parents, who had an export-import business, had a few friends in Zürich who we could tell our parents would watch out for us. It was also centrally located for us to make occasional side trips to other countries if possible. We could work from May through August, and for a few weeks before school resumed back in the States, we could backpack through Italy, which of course, our parents would approve of since both of our mothers were Italian Americans. I knew that Nana still communicated with her nephew Roberto in Rome, who held an important position in the police department. Perhaps, he could keep an eye on us in Italy. My friend's parish priest was in Rome that summer and could also supervise us.

Our strategy was to pay the employment agency $200 each for Switzerland and see what jobs they came up with. Then all we would have to do would be to approach our parents with these options and get approval. We went ahead. One of the jobs was selling refreshments on a train in Switzerland, which we both realized our parents would probably not appreciate. Another option was to work at a hotel in Zürich, the Hotel Carlton Elite. This sounded solid and stable enough to present to the parents. We asked my friend's parents first, who had already raised two older children—sons, both hippies. We knew her parents had already been worn down by them. After dinner one night at their house, we presented our case, and they agreed that if my parents approved, my friend could go. One down, one more really big hurdle to go.

This time I invited my friend to our home for dinner, which, of course, I helped my mother prepare. We had rehearsed our pitch thoroughly. We would begin by talking about how junior year would soon be complete and next year we would successfully graduate from college. She spoke about her parents' business contacts in Switzerland and how she and I were just dying to travel abroad. Next, she told them about the employment agency we found in Manhattan. We had decided that she would initiate the conversation so that, hopefully, my parents would remain calm and that, eventually, I would have to ask the question.

You might think that this is ridiculous because we were both twenty-one years old and college students. In those days that was just not the way things worked. When my sister moved out of the house at thirty years old, and single, my mother said, "An Italian girl doesn't move out of the family home unless she's getting married." Yes, I know, big groan! To my shock and amazement, they listened carefully without yelling at me even once. They interrupted to inquire whether we could afford this venture on our own.

I had expected that question and explained that we had found flights through Montreal to Brussels and ending in Zürich for $99. The hotel would be providing room and board and a small weekly salary. We could purchase inexpensive student rail passes to travel around Switzerland on our days off and that our student IDs would allow us into museums for free. We had also looked into staying at student youth hostels on our excursions which were free. I saved the best for last, explaining that we would be able to work for three months and still have a couple of weeks to travel to Italy, where we could meet our friendly monsignor in Rome and where I intended to visit Nana's beloved nephew Roberto, the police chief. As I had hoped, a look of excitement came over my mother's face at that point, and to my complete shock, they said yes!

We would be joining the throngs of American college students backpacking through Europe in a few short months. Our dreams of seeing the world would be coming true even though we needed a summer job in Europe to make this possible. I got my passport at our local post office and went to downtown Brooklyn to the board of health to obtain a vaccine. Most of all, I remember visiting my beloved Nana to give her the news that I would be going to Italy this summer and that I wanted to visit Roberto.

As soon as possible, I walked over to her apartment a few blocks away, of course, bringing some bread and cookies from her favorite bakery for my visit. Aunt Jennie knew I was coming and had the coffee pot percolating on the stove. My beautiful Nana was sitting in her favorite chair, the pink velvet one in their living room, waiting for me. Now she was seventy-five years old, and her white hair was in a lovely bun with her pretty pearl earrings showing through. She was wearing a sweet floral housedress and little pink leather slides.

After getting a big hug and kiss, she took my hand as I sat on the couch right next to her. I knew that the news I was about to deliver was going to be a big surprise, and I hoped I would also get her blessing. Here was the brave woman who had left her mother and several brothers and sisters at twenty-one years old to travel to a foreign country, never again to return home. She listened intently as I gave her the news, rushing the story to get to the part about wanting to visit Roberto. She was overjoyed that I wanted to visit her favorite nephew, although I could tell she was very nervous about me making such a trip.

I knew that the two of them had corresponded frequently over the years since he had thought of his aunt Christina as being like a mother to him. He had sent her his wedding picture and then pictures of his two little girls. Eventually, he sent her pictures of himself in uniform when he had become a carabinieri—that is, a member of the Italian military police force. Roberto had been successful working as a carabinieri in Rossano, Calabria, and as a result, he was sent with his wife and daughters to Rome for a special assignment and promotion.

For the first time in a long time, I could see a spark of excitement and adventure in my dear grandmother's eyes, and I was delighted to hear her say in her familiar broken English, "Jennie, get my eyeglasses and get my letters from Roberto from *la cache!*" With that, Aunt Jennie opened the hope chest and gathered up the things Nana requested.

To my delight, my grandmother explained that she was going to write me a letter of introduction to bring from her to Roberto in Rome. This was even more than I had expected. I was hoping to get his address and phone number and maybe some hints as to what to say or how to act. Instead, she wrote the most beautiful letter of greetings from her and all the family in Brooklyn to her beloved nephew and explained who the young American girl presenting the letter to him was. After carefully choosing her words, she folded the letter neatly, that she had written in Italian on her special stationery, and placed it in an envelope. She then tucked it in my hand and, placing her own hands over mine, gave me a big kiss and said, "Please take this letter to my dear Roberto and give him these kisses from me."

She also offered to write him another letter immediately, explaining that I would be on my way near the end of August for a trip to Rome with my friend and that I was wishing to meet with him and his family for a brief visit when I was there. She did what she promised the next day and sent the second letter off to Roberto via air mail. Luckily, before I departed for Switzerland in May, we had received a response from Roberto saying that he was excitedly awaiting my visit to him in Rome. I brought Nana's letter of introduction with me on my trip and kept it safe the whole time neatly tucked into my passport. Silly as it may sound, I felt at that time that her letter was a special way for me to help close the family circle which had remained open all those many years.

Chapter Nineteen

My summer abroad was so amazing and enlightening that for the rest of my life I've encouraged young people to travel as soon as possible. The time to go away for an extended period like that is when you're young and you don't have real responsibilities and a mortgage to pay. It opened my mind so much to how the rest of the world lives.

Working in another country gave me a deeper appreciation for the life I lived as an American. We worked like dogs at the hotel with twelve-hour shifts and only a short twenty-minute break for lunch. The pay was measly, but none of that mattered. We lived a few blocks away from the hotel in a building with coworkers, where my friend and I shared a room, and both of us used a bathroom with several other workers. Luckily, we had a little balcony that opened onto the Bahnhofstrasse in Zürich and which gave us a little breathing space. The building had a big loft in the attic where we could all have parties. Most of us working at the hotel were young people coming from countries all around the world, including France, Germany, England, Ireland, Spain, Greece, and Turkey.

As it turns out, at least in 1974, Switzerland was the hotel-management-training capital of the world. Initially, I was assigned to the kitchen, scrubbing pots and pans with an old Italian man, who helped me improve my Italian in preparation for my trip to Italy at the end of the summer. I was a chambermaid for a very strict female Swiss supervisor who seemed to enjoy finding fault with everything we young girls did. I worked in the laundry with an even more difficult younger Swiss supervisor, who bullied me almost all the time and liked to talk about me in Swiss to some Swiss girls working there.

My favorite employment position was working as a barmaid in the hotel's popular café, where I was taught how to use a very complicated coffee/cappuccino/latte machine before fancy coffee was even a thing. I learned how to properly pour draft beer. Making small talk with the customers at the bar and knowing when to give them space was a trick taught to me by one of the older British bartenders. Making conversation was never difficult for me, as you may recall; it was learning when to keep quiet that was my problem. Most of the time, customers were happy to meet me because very few Americans worked at the hotel and the hot topic that summer was the impeachment of President Nixon and, eventually, his resignation.

Most of the day managers at the hotel were Swiss and very tough on us, but there were also a few Germans, who were even more difficult. They did not believe in "the help" socializing with guests at the hotel. We were lucky at the café to usually have a wonderful, jolly older Swiss gentleman, who I will never forget was named Mr. Oetaker. He was of the school of thought that if his people were happy, they would perform their jobs better. He often rewarded us at the end of the closing shift around midnight with a delicious snack for our group, consisting of any of the leftover desserts or sandwiches, and was known to put aside something delicious just for the staff, such as an apricot or rhubarb pie, which we topped off with fresh cream. Somehow, we never got caught even though the hotel general manager, Mr. Sadok, seemed to have eyes everywhere.

We first met Mr. Sadok when we arrived at the hotel after a nearly twenty-four-hour flight. He was surprised to meet two young American college girls dressed in their embroidered jeans, sneakers, and backpacks, who showed up bleary eyed and sleep deprived. Apparently, the agency had given him an incorrect arrival date, so our room was not ready. He had one of the bellboys bring two cots, some pillows, and a blanket to his office and allowed us to sleep there that first night. He gave us a brief pep talk about what he expected of us, such as hard work and discretion, and I could see in his eyes that he didn't expect us to last more than a week. He was friendly and probably felt sorry for us, as we were so exhausted, but I really believed he did not think we had it in us to do the job. This made us even more determined to show him that we weren't spoiled American kids and that we could run circles around the Europeans.

I soon learned that even though we were not spoiled or lazy, we just were not accustomed to working twelve-hour shifts with practically no breaks for what amounted to, back then, about $40 a week (not to mention dealing with a few bullying managers). We worked really hard, and somehow, we did it, eventually earning the respect of not only our supervisors but also all of our coworkers. No one expected these two American college girls to be able to scrub and rub pots, clean and make beds, jump when spoken to, and manage to keep on their feet for so many hours a day or night.

We would save up our day off each week so that we could have a two-day segment to travel around Switzerland and spend our nights in free Alpine youth hostels. I was lucky to make friends with a really cool Swiss girl, Erica, who invited us to her parents' home for the weekend and to her grandmother's chalet up in the Swiss Alps. When we worked in the kitchen, we got to meet some of the young chefs who could occasionally smuggle out a nice bottle of wine or a steak sandwich. By the way, the bottle of wine I was referring to was one which was usually thrown at them by the very temperamental and somewhat alcoholic head chef at the hotel.

As planned, we met the customers of my friend's parents, a

young couple, who owned a really hip record shop in Zürich specializing in jazz music. There also was the luxury car executive, who was another customer of her parents and treated us to a delicious dinner at a fancy restaurant and to a fun night at a beer garden, all things which we never could have afforded back then. One Sunday afternoon, on a Swiss holiday similar to our Fourth of July, he took us out on his sailboat on Lake Zürich. I just kept thinking I must be dreaming!

Near the end of our employment at the hotel, two of our Brooklyn guy friends from school, who were backpacking through Europe themselves that summer, visited us at the hotel, and the four of us made a trip together to another city in Switzerland that weekend. We were thrilled to have two Brooklynites with us, as we were starting to be very homesick. All they could do was talk about their time in Greece and encourage us to go there before we returned home. All we could talk about was what was happening in the States and if they had found any fast-food restaurants on their travels, both of us craving a cheeseburger after three months.

We saw some marvelous sights in Switzerland: gorgeous lakes and Alpine villages, mountains topped with snow in July. We visited many beautiful museums and galleries and found many of the famous places written about in *The Magic Mountain* by Thomas Mann. Eventually, as many of the young people from the other countries returned home once their three-month work visas ran out, we were feeling homesick and realized we actually missed our families. We were unable to afford international telephone calls in those days, and for some reason, all of our mail from home had not reached us for about the first six weeks.

Both of us, when our American friends Glenn and Billy left us, began to seriously look forward to our trip to Italy. We were hoping for an even warmer reception from Italians, especially from the family I was hoping to meet.

Chapter Twenty

We headed off for Italy with our backpacks loaded with some goodies from the hotel kitchen, some T-shirts and jeans, our student rail passes, and an itinerary we had been planning for months. The route was to take the train from Zürich, cross into northern Italy, and head south, stopping at a few select cities along the way, ending in Rome to visit my family, and perhaps one last stop in Naples before heading back north to Zürich. If we liked a city, we would stay a night or two and then move on to the next. We had about three weeks before we needed to be back in Zürich for our return flight home to New York, where our senior year of college awaited us. Immediately, as passengers on the train, we met a different kind of traveler.

The majority of them were Italian. They smiled a lot. They packed picnic lunches and offered some to us. Young Italian soldiers were everywhere, and they especially liked young American girls traveling in their country. One thing I'll never forget about my first trip to Italy in the summer of '74 was that my girlfriend and I always had six or seven Italian soldiers, or carabinieri, following us around. They were almost always nice and friendly, only occasionally getting a little fresh. Yes, Italian men would pinch young girls in those days as a sign of flirting!

Most of them spoke little English, but they gladly offered assistance, and their presence always made us feel safe, which often made us feel flattered but never intimidated or harassed.

I do remember one guy at the beautiful park in Villa Borghese Rome, who asked, in broken English, "Do you girls want to get it on?" but that just made us giggle. They loved that we were both Italian American, at least half Italian, and spoke a little Italian. I remember thinking, *Wow, if a girl ever needs an ego boost, all she had to do was take a trip to Italy!* It got to be our inside joke that if our parents only knew how safe we were with our armored guard, they wouldn't worry about us at all.

After our first fun-filled train ride, we detrained at our first stop, the beautiful and sunny mountaintop, lake-filled city of Como. On a budget of only $10 a day and with the exchange rate in those days of six hundred lire to one dollar, we were easily able to find a small pretty *pensione* with a gorgeous hilltop view of Lago di Como.

Immediately, we changed into our bikinis and ran down to dip into the lake. I had never thought it would be so sunny and warm. I think the warmth came from way deep inside of me because I was finally in Italy, the country my Nana had told me so much about. Something she never told me, however, was that we would be the only women wearing bikini tops at the lakes that summer—the rest of them were topless! And they say American girls are wild!

As much as we enjoyed the beauty and warmth of Como and how all of this city seemed to be focused downward from the cliff tops to the beautiful, crystal-clear lake and as much as we enjoyed their pizza and gelato, we had to shake out of this dreamlike trance and head back to the railroad station if we were going to keep on the itinerary. We hadn't realized how tired we were after working so hard the last three months in Zürich and hiking around as much of Switzerland as possible on our days off. But now refreshed, we were heading toward our next stop, the banking and fashion Mecca of Italy—Milan.

How different this city was from our first stop. We stepped off into a gorgeous station as we exited the train. The streets were paved with marble, lavishly colored peach and green. The vaulted ceilings were glass with views of a rich blue sky. Once outside, we were surrounded by beautiful churches, cathedrals, and a grand cobblestone plaza. Historic buildings housed the most famous and extravagant giants of fashion, like Gucci, Prada, and Versace, and numerous banking institutions paved our way. Again, we found an inexpensive *pensione* with less to offer than the last one. After all, we were in a bigger, more expensive city.

Our $10 a day allowed us to begin our days with delicious cups of espresso accompanied with incredible biscotti or a roll with butter and jam. Lunch was the best pizza we'd ever tasted. For dinner, we would try a local specialty, usually some kind of pasta with a glass of wine, and we always, *always*, finished out the day with some exquisite creamy gelato! In each city, we would find a room near the train station and walk around town from morning to night visiting museums, galleries, parks, and churches.

The next stop for us was the glorious city of Florence, elegant in every way and filled with the most polite and genteel people I had ever met. In Milan and Florence, we noticed how stylishly most of the people were dressed—men in dapper summer linen suits and crisp white shirts and, sometimes, light-colored straw hats. The ladies wore lovely, light-colored dresses, often floral, with pearl necklaces and earrings, and espadrilles completing their outfits. The Duomo and artwork in Florence were unforgettable.

Tipped off by a friendly lady at the train station, we found a very unique place to stay. A middle-aged gentleman was property rich and cash poor, owning a lovely apartment which one entered through an arched doorway in a wall not far from the curb.

Once you stepped in, there was a beautiful courtyard with shade trees and the most fragrant flowers. We walked up a few flights and knocked on the apartment door, only to be welcomed by a slight man about forty, dressed in white and with a brilliant smile.

"Oh, you must be the wonderful young American girls I've heard so much about! Welcome to my palace!" He ushered us into a modest foyer and down a short corridor to our room. It was bright and airy and pristine, with two daybeds, an armoire, a dressing table, and french doors that led out to a tiny balcony. The cost was so reasonable that we could not resist. He insisted that after we cleaned up, we join him in the kitchen for coffee and some fruit so he could assist us in planning our sightseeing.

As he closed the door to the room behind him, we both thought he was either a serial killer and really good at disguising it or just a lonely, down-on-his-luck man. Luckily for us, it was the second guess. We spent about an hour with him in his bright and cheerful kitchen, drinking coffee and eating the summer fruit he had carefully laid out on a pretty blue-and-white-checkered tablecloth.

He had been left this beautiful apartment by his elderly mother. Renting out rooms was his way of making ends meet. We explained that we were college girls on a shoestring budget who had only been able to afford a trip to Europe by working in Switzerland for the last three months.

The three of us clicked immediately. He asked us if we had boyfriends and before we could explain that we were both not ready to seriously settle down, he told us with a huge smile, and while blushing, that he had a boyfriend, which caused the three of us to laugh and to toast his boyfriend with our demitasse coffee cups! Then we excused ourselves, wanting to get in some sightseeing before the end of the day. He gave us a key and wished us good luck, advising us of the quickest route to take to our destination.

We loved every bit of the culture in Florence, especially the Duomo and the Uffizi Gallery, and drooled over the silver and gold jewelry in the many jewelry shops along the Ponte Vecchio, but most of all, I will remember our kind and funny room keeper.

On our last night at his place, he insisted that we have dinner with him, a meal that he would prepare, as he truly enjoyed cooking. We agreed only if he would let us help him in the kitchen. It was one of the best dinners I've ever enjoyed, with lots of wine and pasta in a creamy sauce with summer vegetables, *pasta primavera*. Dessert was a plate of figs and nuts and a tiny side of pistachio gelato because, after all, he was watching his weight. It was difficult to say good-bye the next morning because our stay there felt much more like visiting a relative rather than just renting a room. He insisted that we promise to be careful and safe on the rest of our journey and, especially, to come back to visit him again one day.

Our next stop was and is still my favorite Italian city of all: the jewel on the Adriatic coast, the city of Venice. No matter how I entered the city of Venice—by sea or by railroad—it is one of the most exciting arrivals that I can remember! In 1974, as our train approached Venice, we traveled over a long strip of land like a bridge, and we were surrounded on both sides by the beautiful sea. The city is voluptuous in every way, and immediately one breathes in the salty sea air and your eyes can barely behold the gorgeous vistas. We couldn't wait to board a water-bus so we could be as close as possible to the water and the canals. Venice was hustling and bustling and sundrenched, and the whole time I was there, I felt like I was on a movie set or a fantasy island. This place couldn't be real.

I remember narrow streets filled with vendors and women dropping down baskets on ropes to be filled by the merchants below with their purchases of produce and goods and then pulled up to their apartment balconies. We enjoyed eating alfresco near the canals and walking everywhere. The art galleries were very exciting; my favorite was the Peggy Guggenheim Museum. We took a water taxi to the Isle of Murano to witness the art of the glassblowers. There, I finally found a gift suitable for my favorite uncle and godfather, my Barese-born Uncle Pat! He had gone to Italy once when I was a little girl and brought me back a pretty bracelet. I was determined to find him the perfect gift in Italy. It was a beautiful little multi-colored glass bird that I would safely carry in my backpack and bring back home to him.

My poor Uncle Pat sadly died of cancer just a short time later at the young age of fifty-one. He had contracted cancer as a result of his occupation as a body and fender man, owning a collision shop in Queens near Shea Stadium. I remember visiting my uncle Pat in the hospital where he lay dying of that horrible disease, emaciated and weak, about a year after returning from my trip to Italy. I tried my best not to cry in front of him as I held his hand standing next to my aunt Rosie, who was sitting diligently by his bedside.

I whispered to him, "You're not going to believe this, Uncle Pat, but I just met a boy named Frank a few months ago and we're falling in love! And guess what, Uncle Pat? He's Italian American, and just like you, both sides of his family come from Bari, Italy!"

To which my uncle replied with a huge grin (I always loved his smile). "Bobbie," he began, referring to me by the shortened version of my nickname from Nana, "be careful. If he's falling in love with you, he's going to marry you, and he'll love you forever because that's what Barese men do!" With that, he squeezed my hand, and I gave him a kiss on his cheek before I was ushered out so the rest of the family could come in and say their good-byes. So sadly, my beloved uncle left this world soon thereafter.

Needless to say, I did marry that boyfriend, my Frank, and we are married to this day. Although my beloved godfather never got to meet Frank, I have always felt like I had received his blessing on that last day we were together.

Chapter Twenty-One

A fter Venice, we had planned for two more stops. The first was my long-awaited visit to Rome to meet Nana's dear nephew Roberto and his family, and our final destination would be Naples before it was time to ride the train back to Zürich. I was so excited about finally meeting family in Rome I could hardly sleep a few nights before. *What if they didn't like me? What if I couldn't even find them?* I just wanted to meet them and hug them and give them the kisses Nana would have given them.

I needed to do this for two reasons: First, for myself, because I was really homesick and missing the security, warmth, and love of my family. The second was for my grandmother, who was so excited about my trip, a trip to Italy that she was never able to make herself. I felt like a family ambassador and that, somehow, contact with our Italian family would help to heal my own grandmother's loss and bring her closure to some degree.

After checking into our smallest room yet, we cleaned up, and I wore a special outfit I had been saving for this long-awaited day. We had gotten some instructions on how to get to Roberto's home while at the train station, and as we traveled, we marveled at the grandeur of Rome!

Despite some confusion, we finally located a residential

neighborhood filled with stately apartment buildings. Once again, the building was entered by going through what looks like medieval-arched doors in a wall, opening up to a lovely courtyard. Their apartment was a few flights up, and my heart pounded as we climbed the marble staircase. When we got to their door, I was so excited I thought I might faint from nervousness. I pulled myself together and knocked on the door, not even knowing if anyone would be home. My friend reassured me that everything was going to be okay. I was thinking that, after all, they didn't have a date for our arrival, just an approximation for the beginning of September.

After what seemed like an eternity, a motherly woman opened the door. She was dressed in a cheerful housedress under an apron and her blondish hair was pulled back into a bun. Upon seeing us, her beautiful smile turned into a look of surprise. *Don't tell me*, I thought, *we're in the wrong place or Roberto forgot to tell his family we were on our way!* I immediately pulled my grandmother's letter of introduction from my fringed leather shoulder bag and handed it to the lady, so nervous that I couldn't even speak a word of English, never mind Italian. She had greeted us with some kind of question, but I was also too nervous to understand what she was asking.

As soon as she saw Roberto's name on the front of the envelope and my grandmother's name at the bottom, her eyes opened widely and she pulled the two of us inside the apartment to sit down at the kitchen table. She tore open the letter, and reading quickly, she began to cry. And so, of course, my friend and I began to cry! She quickly jumped up and excused herself and ran to the telephone to call someone whom I assumed would be Roberto, although I couldn't be sure.

After a quick conversation, she returned to us and started hugging us and kissing us and then doing it some more. We spoke a little bit, and I began explaining that I was the granddaughter of Christina LeFosse Longobucco and introduced my friend. She kept nodding her head yes and smiling, and it seemed like she was about to jump for joy. She told us, in a few words, that Roberto was at work, but he would be coming home as soon as possible. She immediately began to make us coffee and I remember that in her excitement, she actually kept putting spoons full of sugar into our little espresso cups. It's so funny how one can remember such little details of such a special old memory. She offered us some cookies and invited us to step outside onto a little balcony and take in a gorgeous view of Rome.

Before too much time had passed, two young giggling girls entered the apartment carrying bags of groceries. After they exchanged a few words, I soon learned from the younger one of the girls, named Silvana, who spoke a little English, that I had been speaking to their mother, Roberto's wife, Rosetta. She said they were their daughters, Anna and Silvana, one who was one year older than me and the other one year younger. The girls were so beautiful and friendly and, to me, seemed so fascinating. They joined us at the table for coffee, where we all laughed and smiled from ear to ear eating cookies until Rosetta began to politely prepare an afternoon lunch.

The girls said they had just returned from a family vacation to Calabria, which was their habit during the summertime to escape the heat of Rome. Silvana explained that they had been so excited for my visit, and their father was even more so. The girls peppered us with lots of questions about our trip to Switzerland and Italy and seemed to be astonished that girls their own age would not only take such a trip but that our parents would have permitted it. They asked us about America and fashion and music—all the things young people are interested in everywhere.

I learned, eventually, during our visit over the next few days, that their father, who was a police chief in Rome, was very strict, just like most fathers in Italy. They explained that after dinner, even if they just wanted to go out for a stroll, the whole family went, the girls walking ahead and their mama and papa following behind. We had observed this tradition as we traveled around Italy and I remember it being called *una passeggiata*.

Just like young girls do, we talked and talked and talked until suddenly the apartment door opened again, and in walked a handsome middle-aged man in a beige summer suit with a huge smile and open arms! That's when we all started crying again!

Roberto read my grandmother's letter that Rosetta handed to him and was grinning from ear to ear as tears rolled down his cheeks. He asked many questions about my grandmother, his dear aunt, and us and the rest of the family. He explained that Nana was like a mother to him, having lost his own mother, Anna, when he was so young. He excused himself to wash before lunch, and as we readied the table to eat, he put on some beautiful Italian music. He announced that since today was such a momentous occasion, we were going to enjoy some special wine and bread that they had brought back from their trip to Calabria. He said that even though my journey had brought me to Rome and not actually to Calabria, where we were all originally from, this special bread and wine would be a fitting addition to our meal. We sat around the table eating and laughing and talking as Roberto asked us so many questions about our work in Zürich, our travels in Switzerland, and our journey to Rome.

He was impressed to hear that we were both college girls and would be finished with school next year. He wanted to know about our parents and siblings, and so for about an hour, we shared as much as we could. He announced that he would not have to return to work this evening and asked about our luggage. When I explained that we had left our things at a *pensione*, he was disappointed and insisted that we go gather our belongings and sleep at their place the next couple of nights. I didn't feel comfortable imposing on them and assured him that we were fine staying at the *pensione*.

The only way he would agree to this arrangement was if we could spend as much time together, at least with his wife and daughters, for the next couple of days and only if he could drive us back to our *pensione* that night to check it out and give his approval.

"Okay, okay, *multo bene*," I said. They all laughed any time I spoke Italian, and Silvana explained that they did not mean to make fun of me but that they couldn't understand how this American girl was speaking Italian in a Calabrese dialect! I knew people in Italy spoke many different dialects and explained that I never studied Italian in school but that I had learned Italian from my grandmother. Then I said, "Nana spoke to me in Italian, and I answered her in English, so excuse me if my Italian is mixed up." To explain further, I continued, "I speak Italian like a *giambotta*!" Everyone laughed again because that's a Calabrese peasant-style dish of mixed fresh vegetables and potatoes that our family loves to cook in the summertime, hoping that they would understand how mixed up my Italian really was!

We then went outside to walk around the neighborhood and stroll through their local piazza and ended up taking our own *passeggiatta* with all of us girls strolling arm in arm while Roberto and Rosetta walked closely behind us. After a nice tour of the neighborhood, where they pointed out some churches and historic sites, Roberto bought us some gelato, and we ate sitting at a nearby fountain. He informed us that we would walk back to his place so he could get his car and drive us to the *pensione* for his inspection. We also planned to meet the girls at the Coliseum and Roman Forum the next morning so they could take us on a day tour.

Roberto and Rosetta insisted that, in two nights, we must return to their home. He was planning a party for that evening, and he was inviting some other family in Rome and a few friends. Of course, we agreed, and after driving to the *pensione* and Roberto's meeting with the owner of the establishment and checking out our room, we said good night to Roberto with more hugs and kisses!

The next couple of days were a whirlwind of sightseeing, fun, and laughter. Silvana and Anna were such fun to be with, and we eventually got to meet Anna's fiancé. Both my friend and I felt like we had known these two girls all of our lives and so enjoyed their company. We were laughing about how impressed

Roberto was that one of those few days together, we met with the monsignor from my friend's parish back in Brooklyn. The monsignor was very friendly with my friend's parents and was in Rome on business. He had promised her parents he would meet us for dinner and check on us. The girls told us that Roberto felt more comfortable knowing some "big shot" priest was somehow "watching over us," but we never mentioned to Roberto all the young Italian carabinieri who had also been watching over us on our Italian adventure.

Then there was the big farewell party! It was a magical evening in the courtyard of their home. Roberto and Rosetta and the girls had planned a wonderful party for us with several of their guests and had prepared so many dishes of Italian delicacies. We laughed, and we told stories about our family and about our trip and ate and drank so much that I thought I would never eat again!

Near the end of the night, when just a few of us remained, my cousins Anna and Silvana made a request of their parents, asking if they would be permitted to travel with us to Naples and return with us to Rome on our way back to Zürich. The girls had been asking us to help hatch this plan, but I could see immediately that their father was not going to allow it. Instead, we made a promise to meet again one day when we were older, and then we could continue our adventure together. Anna and Silvana had become so dear to me in such a short time, and I promised to always keep in touch with them.

Tearfully, we all embraced, and Roberto gave me a letter to take home to my grandmother, sent with abundant love. He warned us of the dangers of Napoli, advising us to be extra careful. He explained that the streets were full of pickpockets and to call him if there were any problems. Rosetta gave us a little bundle of goodies to enjoy on the train ride in the morning, and she and the girls hugged and kissed us some more, enough to last until we all met again. Roberto drove us back to the *pensione* and waved good-bye to us with tears in his eyes.

Chapter Twenty-Two

We boarded a train and headed south to our last destination: the city of Naples. We couldn't help but laugh at all of the warnings we had been given about the pickpockets and thieves we might encounter there, even from my grandmother back in Brooklyn. People used to call the young little pickpockets in Naples, *scoonyeets*. But we were not afraid. After all, how bad could Naples be? I mean, we grew up in Brooklyn and were used to crime and muggings. So, we laughed it off and exited the train.

Immediately, we were approached by a nicely dressed gentleman who had been sitting in the same car as us and smiling as he listened to us laughing about the warnings. As we were walking out of the station, he came over to us and said, "*Seniorini, guardano i tuoi portafogli tenerli strettamente sotto le braccia*, okay?" (*Young ladies, watch your pocketbooks and keep them under your arms, okay?*). All the while, he pointed with much enthusiasm toward our purses and out toward the street. Okay, so now this was starting to get a little worrisome.

We walked out into the street and, finding a *pensione* that required a short bus ride, we headed out to find it. Boarding a very crowded bus, we squeezed onto it and decided we had to stand back to back to each other, so that little prying hands could not get into our packs. (As I'm writing this, I'm wondering if I'll be sued by Naples, but I swear all of this is true.)

We arrived at the *pensione*, where an unfriendly older woman stared us up and down and took us to a room with two small fold-up beds, which we accepted. The next thing you know, she demanded our passports, and as we were hesitant to turn them over, she took out a bar of soap and, taking our passports, she said in Italian, "When you give me back the soap, I will give you back your passports!" *Okay, now I guess we won't take too many showers!* We dropped off our backpacks and decided to head out for dinner by the ocean and to scout out a way to visit the isle of Capri by boat the next day.

As we trotted down a hill of cobblestone streets, we were in the midst of a lot of commotion. All the doors of businesses were wide open with people shopping all around us. At one point, we saw a very tall muscular young man doing carpentry work. Peeking into the store, we saw he was making coffins. We continued on, looking for a nice place to eat at the shore. Suddenly, encountering a small group of young boys who started teasing and following us, our smiles faded quickly as they started to throw small firecrackers at us!

We ran away from them and narrowly made it, safely, to a nearby restaurant. Since it was only early evening and the sun had not yet set, the place was empty except for the two of us. Italians eat a late dinner at about 8:30 p.m. We ordered some cheap white wine and pasta with seafood, which tasted very good but also very salty. Wondering if something was wrong, we inquired about the saltiness and the waiter told us that they cooked with water that was just like the sea.

We finished up and decided to find a small tour boat that might take us to Capri. We walked along the shoreline, filled with lots of boats, looking for some kind of tour boat but instead found plenty of fishing boats filled with young men. They all offered to take us to Capri with nice big smiles, remarking that it would be their pleasure! Following our Brooklyn instincts, we headed back to our *pensione* before it got too dark and thought we'd make an alternate plan for the next day.

We undressed and settled on our cots and opened the windows to get some cool air, as it was a pretty warm evening in September. We fell asleep as the rest of Naples woke up. It sounded like they were having a feast out on the streets. Somehow, we managed to pass out, but about an hour or two later, when it had gotten quite late, there was banging on our door.

We woke up startled, and before we could get to the door, in walked our landlady with two young men who told us to get out of our beds, which they quickly folded up and rolled out of the room, and then proceeded to open up a pullout couch for us to sleep on. That was enough for us—we were getting the next train out of Naples. We dressed in the dark and stalled until six a.m. when we knocked on the landlady's door with the soap in our hands. We paid for the room for one night and she handed us back our passports after taking back her bar of soap.

We made it back to the train station as the sun was rising and while the streets were pretty empty. The two of us began to laugh and decided that everyone had been right. Naples was a rough and crazy city! Luckily, an alternate plan came up as we saw signs to Ischia and Breschia. So that's where we headed out for another day or two, enjoying two seaside towns, filled with lots of wealthy tourists and outdoor cafés, lots of sunshine and beach, and all the gelato we could eat.

Then we finally boarded a train to return to Zürich, back to the Hotel Carlton Elite and our Swiss friends who'd be waiting to hear all our stories. To this day, if anyone asks if I've ever been to Naples or if I want to go to Naples, I remember why when Italians are arguing and want to tell you to go to hell, they say, *"Vai al Napoli!"*

After a long train ride back, we had a couple of days to get ourselves organized, pick up our last paycheck, and report to the police department (yes, with our working visas in those days, we were required to report to the police station every so often).

We had only a little money left to treat ourselves to a nice hair salon, where we both decided to chop off some of our wild, hippie hair and get European hairstyles.

Then on the last night, we found a note on our door inviting us up to the attic quarters, where a surprise farewell party was waiting for us, given by a few of the remaining young people who were still working at the hotel. We toasted each other and laughed and danced and laughed some more. At one point, another American girl—Zoe from upstate New York—who had recently arrived at the hotel, came over to tell us she was not going back home to finish college. She had fallen madly in love with one of the young waiters and they were going to be married soon! We hugged and kissed her and wished her the best.

Even though my friend and I had been tempted to stay in Europe, skip school, and keep traveling, we had not considered it that seriously. It would be hard to go back home to live with our parents and under their rules after a summer of complete freedom, but we were both seriously homesick and determined to finish college. Besides, I couldn't wait to tell Nana all about my trip to Italy and my visit with her special nephew Roberto and his lovable family.

Chapter Twenty-Three

I was so happy to be home with everyone I loved, but it was a little difficult to adjust to my parents' rules and curfews again after a summer of freedom and a little bit of wilding. Gone were the days of three dates in one day, each with a boy from a different country. Things quieted way down anyway, now that I was no longer a novelty — that is, I was no longer one of only three American girls working at the hotel. I was back in good-old Brooklyn, and school started almost as soon as we returned.

My first order of business was to decide what path my professional life was going to take. I had wanted to become a doctor since my early teens and throughout high school, enthusiastically joining the BioMed Club. I was always fascinated with science — math not so much. I also loved writing and other liberal arts.

Amazingly, I won a place in a six-year BA–MD program when I started Brooklyn College, which meant that college was completed in three years, then on to Down State Medical School. I was thrilled, but as soon as we started orientation for the program at Brooklyn College, I became immediately intimidated. I felt that most of the other students in the program, who were from public schools, seemed to have a far superior background in science. My high school lab was ancient and seriously lacking in up-to-date equipment.

My first course of biology laboratory was very frightening to me, as I barely recognized much of the equipment and saw how familiar my classmates were with them. Luckily, I became friends with a smart, sweet Jewish girl named Miriam Greenbaum. She had just returned from a kibbutz in Israel and seemed so mature and intelligent to me. She and I became study buddies, but no matter how hard I worked, I only managed to get a B in the course, which for me at that time was unacceptable.

On the other hand, I relished the liberal arts classes I was taking, particularly philosophy. I had no problem keeping up with the reading, and writing papers came naturally to me. When I tried to get some guidance from my family about my choice to become a doctor, they would always say, "Whatever you want to do is great with us." When I went to high school, I never had a guidance counselor. They told us we could do whatever we wanted to as young women, when things back then were so different and it was thought that just going to college was amazing enough.

My parents had me speak to my great-aunt Mabel, who had been a nurse for many years. Although she encouraged me to go for it if becoming a doctor was my dream, she, along with my mother, would say things like, "But if you become a nurse, it will be so much easier to have a family and raise children."

I even spoke with my mother's cousin Johnny, a grandson of Aunt Victoria, who had been very successful in college, first becoming a pharmacist and then going to medical school in Bologna, Italy. Here he was a brilliant Brooklyn guy, who spoke our Calabrese dialect and still had to struggle with the language barrier as the courses there were taught in what was called "high Italian." Again, he was encouraging but not very enthusiastic, as the road for him had been very difficult and expensive.

I also heard from many of the students in the program at Brooklyn College that they were having difficulty being accepted into residency programs, and many had to apply to Mexico. None of this did anything to boost my confidence. I was still that crazy little kid that wasn't satisfied or happy unless I was at the top of my class, feeling that anything else was never good enough.

So in my freshman year, looking at my B in biology and A in philosophy, I walked over to the philosophy department one afternoon, without consulting my parents or any of the professors in my special program at the college, and declared philosophy as my major and then walked over to the other side of the campus and withdrew from that BA–MD program. I was so relieved by my decision and thoroughly enjoyed the rest of my college years. I didn't tell my parents about this choice until months after, and once again they said something like, "Whatever you decide, we back you one hundred percent!" My parents were the best, and they always made us feel so loved.

With graduation approaching, I needed a plan. I finally decided to seek the advice of a wonderful professor in the philosophy department who had already helped me so much. Professor Brown had been exceptionally understanding for the last three years and always offered constructive advice. He even recommended me for a special philosophy department award. It was his suggestion that I apply to grad school. If I wished to continue in the field of philosophy, a master's degree would be required. At least this time I followed someone's advice, and I nervously applied to NYU's graduate school. I was thrilled to find out I was accepted, this time with a full fellowship! I was finally going to the school of my dreams, which had been too expensive for my family four years before.

So off I went to NYU, of course, still living at home. Now, classes were really difficult, but the professors were brilliant and my courses so inspiring. And here I was finally going to school in Greenwich Village. Most of the classes were at night, so I supported myself at first as a salesgirl and eventually as a bank teller, thanks to a friend of the new boy I was dating.

The young man I had told my uncle about and I soon fell in love, and after I graduated from Brooklyn College, he asked me to marry him. I happily said yes, but told him not until after I graduated from NYU. I was afraid I might get distracted and possibly lose the fellowship that was making this all possible for me.

After working hard for three years and successfully completing my master's thesis, which was approved by three of the professors in the philosophy department, I was done! Frank and I married, and he and my mother were able to attend my graduation ceremony, which was held at Washington Square Park on a beautiful June day. I will never forget the loving look on my mom's face as she saw me walk by her in a procession of graduates in my cap and gown. I kept thinking, *This is for you, Mom.*

The only problem was, how would I get a job in my field? My father asked me what they should get a philosophy student for graduation—a toga? I had a meeting with the really cool head of the department, who was a jazz musician on the side. He could be heard playing his sax in his office down the hallway from the student advisor's office. I consulted with him when I first began their graduate program, and he welcomed me and gave me some advice on how to survive in graduate school. I saw him again when it was time to discuss my master's thesis and he assigned an advisory professor to me. Now we were discussing job options in my field, and when I explained that my husband's job with the city of New York required him to live within the city limits, he explained that finding a job as a philosophy professor within the city of New York would be almost impossible without having a doctorate's degree. *Here I go again!*

When I got home that night, my husband and I had a long talk about how we could work this out while still living in our "cozy" three-room apartment in the old Brooklyn neighborhood. At twenty-four, I was school weary and decided to take a year off and kept working at my bank-teller job until I could find something more suitable. He had a great job in law enforcement with the opportunity for lots of overtime. We both needed to save money before I could go back to school full time.

In a few months, I found out from a fellow bank teller, who also was a recent college graduate, that a downtown Manhattan law firm was hiring young college graduates to be something called "paralegals." This was new to me and apparently new in the field of law as well. I jumped at the chance to earn more money and after an arduous interview at a famous white-collar law firm—Lord, Day, and Lord—in downtown Manhattan on Broadway, I was hired. I felt like a fish out of water. No one had a last name like mine or looked like me or dressed like me.

Thankfully, my friend was hired too, and she was in the know, having a boyfriend who attended law school. I quickly caught on and, with our measly budget, bought a few outfits suitable for this type of firm, cut my hair, and paired up with another young woman, Mary, who was a newlywed too.

After about a year or so, my new friend begged me to take the LSATs with her. She was lucky to have an older brother who was an attorney, and she saw this as a logical next step. I had never even thought about going to law school. On a whim, I discussed it with my husband to see if we even had enough money to pay an application fee. "Go for it, babe," he said. Almost as a joke, and trying to help my friend who really wanted to go to law school, I agreed to take the exam, and we bought LSAT review books so we could study together during our lunch.

Then, life took a turn, and unfortunately, my sweet friend lost her dad suddenly from a heart attack. Comforting her, I assured her we would just take the LSAT the next time it was offered. But she insisted I go ahead and take it myself now; she said that would make her happy. What was I supposed to do? Take a test I never wanted to take for a profession I had no interest in? That's what I did. To my surprise, I managed to get a decent score. Now, something that started as a lark was becoming real.

There were two young attorneys at the firm I did paralegal work for whom I really admired, so I decided to ask their advice.

Both of them had attended Brooklyn Law School and raved about it, especially because its graduates had a very high percentage of passing the New York State Bar exam. They were very impressed with the fact that I already had a master's degree from NYU and told me I would be crazy not to apply there. They also offered to write recommendations to the school for me. How could I say no?

My husband once again said, "Go for it, babe," and the next thing I knew, I was sitting in a large first-year law school classroom filled mostly with men and feeling way over my head. It was a great school with impressive and caring professors, and I made several lifelong friends there, one of whom would eventually become one of my law partners and best friends, but to be honest, I hated law school! It was the most competitive place I had ever found myself in, and the workload was extremely difficult. Those were the days of grueling hours and hours of actual time spent in a library and so much reading and studying to be done, never mind the daily stress of never knowing when you would be randomly called on to participate in verbal sparring with a professor. Oh yes, the famous Socratic method.

To make matters worse, attending law school full time and feeling like I was winging it was even more stressful for me because I had no one in my personal life I could go to for advice or direction. I didn't know anyone who went to law school. In my first year, it seemed like everyone had a family member or friend who was a lawyer or a judge. I found myself too embarrassed to ask classmates for help, as I was already a few years older than most of them. It was also difficult to keep up with family obligations. Thankfully, my husband, my parents, and all of my family were very proud of me and supportive, but I couldn't help feeling guilty about not having the time to spend with them.

As my first semester was drawing to a close and I began to study for my first final exams, just when I was feeling the most anxious, my dear grandmother Christina—Nana—became very sick with congestive heart disease. I tried to visit her since she only lived a few blocks from the tiny apartment where my husband and I lived, but it was heartbreaking. She could barely keep her eyes open, sleeping most of the time and not able to speak much. She would gesture to me to sit on the bed next to her and to hold her hand and sometimes to close my eyes and lay my head on the pillow next to her. She would say to me, "Bobbie, close your eyes, take a rest. You work too hard," as she quietly fell asleep. I would stare for a while at the beautiful little altar on her dresser with the statue of the Blessed Mother and remember how she would let me light the candles when I was a little girl before climbing into bed with her. Nowadays, I would wait until she dozed off and, kissing her hand or her cheek, tiptoe out of her room and then run to my apartment to study.

Sadly, the night before my last final exam, my mother called and told me that Nana had been taken by ambulance to the hospital and had been admitted. Aunt Anna and Aunt Jennie had stayed with her there to watch over her. I don't know how I got through the last of my final exams the next morning, but I raced out of school in downtown Brooklyn and hopped on a subway back home to Borough Park. Once there, I called my mom who told me that she and my aunts were at her home having a quick lunch and a little rest, exhausted from the night before.

"Okay, Mom, no worries, I'm jumping in my car and heading right now to see Nana at the hospital!"

I ran into her room, only to find her extremely upset and crying, as she was breathlessly trying to communicate with the young nurse in Italian, which, of course, the nurse did not understand. Even though her English had improved so much over the years, I'm sure since she was feeling so sick and scared, she could only remember what she was trying to say in her native Italian. Seeing me, she stopped crying and reached out to hug me after throwing her hands up in the air as if thanking God for sending someone from the family to her rescue. We calmed her down, and I translated for the nurse, who then left the room to go get her medication. I helped Nana lie back comfortably in her hospital bed, and she beckoned me to sit next to her and hold her hand. I watched her as she began to doze off, so thankful I had gotten there just in time.

What happened next was one of the worst things I've ever experienced and one which I will never forget. Shortly thereafter, the nurse returned with the medication. My grandmother was woken up so the nurse could administer the pills. It seemed like not even five minutes after the nurse had left the room that my grandmother started to go into convulsions. I panicked and began to call for help while trying to hold my grandmother so she wouldn't fall out of the bed. Immediately, hospital personnel came running into the room with a crash cart as I heard them calling a code blue over the loudspeaker. I don't know what happened next because they quickly ushered me out of the room.

I waited, in shock, in the hallway for someone to come tell me what was going on. Finally, they asked me to wait a bit until I could see Nana again. I was allowed to call my mother so she and my aunts could come to the hospital. Everyone from the nearby family came, and little by little we were allowed to spend a couple of minutes with my grandmother who had suffered a stroke and was unable to speak to any of us.

By nighttime, the doctor advised us to go home to rest and promised he would call with any updates. As happens time and time again, once everyone finally got home, the doctor called my aunt Anna with the terrible news that my grandmother had died. My heart was broken when I found out Nana was gone. *How could I go on living without her?* We were all devastated. Our brave and beautiful family matriarch, who had journeyed to America at twenty-one years old, was gone at eighty-one years old. We all felt lost without her.

Chapter Twenty-Four

I don't know how I pulled myself together after the short school break to begin the spring semester of my first year of law school. I was tired and sad and felt even more stressed out than ever. All I could do to cope was dive into my work and try to imagine that my grandmother was still with me, with all of us. I shoved my feelings aside because there was too much at stake. I put one foot in front of the other and got lost in the difficult work before me. Work can be numbing, and in this case, it definitely was for me.

That spring, moot court was added to our already difficult workload. Arguing and competing during many rounds of moot court and then several internships during law school made me realize this was what I was born to do. I was no longer limited to the work expected of me. I could be passionate about my profession and become financially independent at the same time!

The rest of the three years flew by. I filled each summer with exposure as an intern to various legal fields. Although as a student intern I didn't earn a penny, I did earn credits, and the mentors I met were invaluable to me, helping shape my future in the law immeasurably!

When the New York State Bar exam finally came upon me, I knew enough to enroll in a bar review course. My best friend and law-school colleague and I, both assuming we would never find jobs, having no connections in the legal world, came up with a plan. We were both newlyweds and both Italian American women coming from family-oriented backgrounds—if no one would hire us, we would just start our own all-female law firm! We had met as moot-court partners and respected each other's work ethics completely. Believing that two heads were better than one, we figured we could work it out.

To our surprise, we were both offered excellent jobs during the first round of interviews at our law school. I was offered a job as an Assistant District Attorney at Kings County, being hired by the first woman to ever be elected as District Attorney of Brooklyn, Elizabeth Holtzman. I actually found out I was the very first person she even hired to be an Assistant DA. That year, 1982, felt like the year of the woman. She was impressed with the firm where I had served as a paralegal, knowing many of the partners there, and she was interested in the research I had done as a student clerk to a federal judge in the Southern District of New York since it involved actual legislation she had been involved with as a congresswoman.

Although I had secretly been seeking a position at the city of New York's Corporation Counsel, where I had been engaged also as a student intern, I decided to take the job at the DA's office because, as they say, "A bird in the hand . . ." Ironically, my friend received an offer from the New York City Corporation Counsel, which she happily accepted. We decided we would put our dream of starting our own law firm on hold for a while so we could gain excellent experience in both the criminal and civil fields and finally get paid for it. That way, we would have a good foundation to start our own firm in the future. Right now, student loans needed to be paid off!

My five years as an Assistant District Attorney in Brooklyn were the best years of my professional life. I treasure the experience I received there, both as a trial attorney and as a supervisor. It was rough and tough, both mentally and physically, working crazy hours and holidays since New York City crime and courts never sleep. The bonds that were developed with my coworkers have lasted a lifetime. You cannot survive that type of job without the help of supervisors and other assistant district attorneys.

We were fighting a war in good-old lawless Brooklyn in those days. For a girl who was born and bred in Brooklyn, this job was truly a dream come true. My parents, husband, and family could not be prouder of me and, on occasion, came to observe me in the courtroom. There were no other lawyers in our family, and my mom and dad never missed an opportunity to tell just about anyone they met—something that always began like this, "Well, my daughter the lawyer . . ." And although embarrassing at first, I must admit, I always loved hearing them say that!

I treasure the many times I appeared before a judge in the Criminal Court of Kings County or a justice of the Supreme Court of Kings County and heard a court officer announce loudly, "All rise, the Honorable Judge (or Justice), _____, now presiding!" The judge or justice would then inquire, "Are the People ready for trial?" To which I would proudly respond, "The People of the County of Kings are ready for trial, Your Honor!"

These were rough-and-tumble days of trial work, where you had to be quick on your feet and prepared for anything to happen (and it did) at the last minute. The class of prosecutors of '82 had to work diligently, always remembering we were duty-bound to see that justice was done. One bureau chief reminded us that we were like champions of the people of Kings County, appearing in court on our daring steed and waving a banner for truth and justice. We often encouraged each other after a few of our first trials with earning the title of "trial animal" as a way to alleviate the enormous stress of those days!

We had excellent training from our supervisors, worked twenty-four-hour shifts in the Investigations Bureau, and met detectives in some of the worst precincts in Brooklyn to conduct line-ups and take statements of suspects who wanted to confess. Since we were in New York City, you never knew who you might meet in a courtroom—whether famous or notorious, celebrity or pariah—either as a defendant or defense attorney. Once, I was in an elevator in the courthouse with famous attorney William Kunstler, and I had to restrain myself from being a ridiculous "fangirl" over him!

Eventually, I went on to start the first all-women's law firm on Staten Island with my law school friend in 1987. It was very difficult breaking into the old boys' club there, but we chipped away at it, bit by bit, client by client, joining the various local bar associations and making friends. We even helped grow a newly founded Staten Island Women's Bar Association.

Now that I was initially doing mostly criminal defense work, I was having a very difficult time getting appointed to what was called the "18B felony criminal defense panel." It was not due to my credentials—I had more trial experience than many other attorneys applying for the same panel—but I was a woman and an outsider, coming from Brooklyn. Staten Island, at least at that time, had maybe one female judge that I can recall. It was a much more conservative borough than Brooklyn.

Thanks to the understanding and help of a kind and supportive Richmond County Supreme Court Justice, who was himself very proud of the accomplishments of his own daughters, I was finally assigned to cases by him, and naturally, admission to the panel shortly followed. When I first tried a case in that court, he told me I was the first woman ever to try a criminal case at the felony level for the defense on Staten Island. It was a moment of pride for me, and yet, at the same time, I felt disappointed that it had taken so long for this to happen; it was 1988.

Chapter Twenty-Five

I never thought my life could get more hectic than when I worked in the DA's office, but I soon found that having my own practice would keep me busy 24/7. It was challenging and rewarding beyond belief. I had found so much satisfaction in my work and in helping my clients that it partially became an outlet for my maternal instincts.

I went through a stressful time trying to have children for about ten years, seeking fertility doctors all over New York City. Nothing seemed to work, and yet everything worked for my friends. I tried it all and have no regrets except that, perhaps, I should have embarked on this journey when I was a few years younger.

In those days, insurance covered none of the doctors or treatments, medications, or surgeries. IVF was brand new when I needed it, and I was rejected from a famous program in Manhattan due to my particular hormonal problem and because I think, initially, they were only looking for optimal candidates for their statistics. Adoption was too scary for me. We were going through a period at the time when adoptions were first "open" and surrogacy was being challenged. Was it bad timing? For me, it was. My exposure as an attorney in family court did even more to scare me off, and so after ten years of all kinds of treatments, procedures, surgeries, and fertility drugs, I gave up. The last fertility drug I used via injection was made from the urine of nuns from Italy, costing $1,000 a month, which resulted in my undergoing a complete and total hysterectomy at age forty. It was not meant to be. Or was I another victim of the family curse? It didn't matter. The result was the same.

I cherished my profession as an attorney and was more than rewarded by the results I was able to achieve for my clients, many of whom had no one else in their lives to advocate for them. Then there was this big, lovable family of mine and my supportive and devoted husband, which I realized, in time, more than compensated for being unable to have a child. This was the time in my life when I finally realized that no one has everything and you were lucky to be blessed with having someone who loved you, whether or not it was a spouse or child, or anyone else for that matter.

At about this time, my loving Italian American Brooklyn family had gone through many changes. Both of my dear uncles, brothers Tony and Pat, had died very young, leaving my aunts Inez and Rosie widows with children to support. The heart of our family, my dear Nana, had left us. The family started to scatter to other boroughs and suburbs outside of New York City, and many of us cousins began to marry.

My aunts, Anna and Jennie, moved into a nice, new senior-citizen residence on Shore Road in Brooklyn.

My brother's first marriage unfortunately was short-lived. He took a job as a contractor working for the Federal Savings and Loan Association after a recession on Wall Street, where he formerly worked in the late eighties and early nineties. Eventually, he fell in love and married a sweet young woman, Debbie, from Alabama, and they had a beautiful baby girl, Annie, which added to their blended family of two other adorable little girls, Brooke and Brittany.

My parents, my sister, and I visited my brother and his family many times where they settled in Georgia, as we missed him and all fell in love with his first baby girl, who was my parents' first grandchild, and his two stepdaughters who immediately became daughters, nieces, and granddaughters to all of us in the Gomes family. Even though a move to Georgia seemed like a giant leap to us Brooklynites, we fell in love with the weather, the people, and the way of life in the South. The main draw was to live closer to my brother and his wonderful family. My sister was the first to decide to join him. Opportunities for a single girl in the South were attractive, and with her experience working as a legal secretary in some of the top-notch New York law firms, she had no problem finding a good job there.

My parents were approaching retirement. They had worked so hard all their lives doing everything for their children and now it was their time to relax. They never went on vacations without their kids and scrimped and saved for their children's future. Even though my old-fashioned mother had a hard time accepting that my single sister had moved to Georgia, she hesitated to make the move there herself. I remember her asking me, "Barbara, is your sister mad at me? Did she tell you what's wrong?"

"What are you talking about, Mom? She's not mad at you!"

And again, "Well, you know, Italian American girls don't move out of their parents' home to get their own place unless they're getting married."

Oh boy, I thought, *my sister is thirty years old and could afford her own beautiful place in the South and enjoy the warmer climate for her health, and my old-fashioned mom is on a completely different wavelength.*

My father, on the other hand, was totally energized by the thought of joining my brother, his family, and my younger sister in Georgia, where his Social Security checks could go a long way. He figured he and my mom could find a pretty, little house on a small, wooded piece of property. Was I chopped liver? To be left all alone in New York by the rest of them?

All kidding aside, no one was expecting me to leave my firm

on Staten Island and my husband to leave his successful career in New York City. However, the differences in my parents' retirement dreams were very drastic and caused much bickering between the two of them. This was a time when I was asking myself, *How did these two ever get married and make it last for forty-four years?* My dad was looking forward to a change and challenge, and my mom had no desire to leave her beloved Brooklyn nor her house in Dyker Heights, which gave her all the security and pride that she never had as a poor little girl growing up. She and her sisters and Nana were always being forced to move from apartment to apartment at the landlord's whim.

It seemed that my parents had completely different views on how to spend their golden years. My dad was feeling vibrant and young again, ready for adventure, while my mom was worried to make a big move and thought he was being unreasonable.

My mom threatened to go live with her two single sisters, Anna and Jennie, and said that my dad could go to Georgia without her. In retrospect, I think it was a combination of how they each viewed retirement and that my mother had a serious case of empty-nester syndrome. My father had taught me that change is a good thing and that one must anticipate change and act accordingly instead of waiting too late until the change was forced upon you.

My mother, however, would not budge. Eventually, after some marriage counseling and heart-to-heart conversations, and dealing with issues that had too long been neglected, my parents, Annie and Bill, came out with a new perspective and, surprisingly, were like a young couple madly in love again.

My parents, my husband, and I began the long process of cleaning out the house where they had lived for over forty years to make it ready to sell. The chore seemed impossible and never-ending. Going through all of my parents' belongings, and many of those of my brother and sister and also mine, was bittersweet. The twelve-room house was just too much for them at their age and needed too much repair and renovation. It was almost one hundred years old at the time and needed a young family to give it new life.

The house was barely on the market a week or two when an offer was made by a nice young couple with two small children, and they were an Italian American family! As you can imagine, that sealed the deal. So now my father was looking forward to his little southern cottage in the woods where he could sit out on the back deck and enjoy bird watching, which he announced would be his new hobby, and playing with his grandchildren whenever he was not doing the former. This came from a man who had worked for many years in retail, six days a week, working very hard, twelve-hour days while standing on his feet, and he was really showing his age.

My mom, who had gone back to work outside the home once my sister had grown up, had worked at a bank in customer service and taken so seriously every customer's demand. She learned at an older age how to work with computers and would take work home to study for the next day. When her job in Brooklyn at a local bank had been eliminated, to our surprise, she took the option to work in their Manhattan branch, requiring her to take buses and subways in her senior years while she was not in the best of health. She had even worked an additional year past sixty-five in order to keep my father covered with her medical insurance. She now had visions of a newer home, full of all the conveniences she could imagine—without stairs and where she could pick and choose all the appliances and doodads she had wanted for her kitchen.

Again, life was good. Well, at least it was for a couple of days.

Chapter Twenty-Six

J ust when everything was looking up and my mom and dad were like a young couple again, madly in love and excited about their years ahead together, all hell broke loose. It felt as if they were jinxed, as we used to say, or that the old family curse had come back to haunt us.

I was visiting my mom on a beautiful autumn afternoon just before Halloween and found her reading a big thick book and drinking her instant coffee. She never read any average or typical library books. They were always big, fat ones, like Bibles. Seeming a little down and nervous about the house sale, I asked when she had last gone out of the house to get some fresh air.

"Mom, you can't stay in the house all the time, you need to get outside, in the sunshine—you're starting to look yellow!" Since I was always one to exaggerate, my mom shook her head in annoyance and took another drag of her cigarette. "I'm not kidding, I'm driving you to Caesar's Bay. We can buy some Halloween treats and cards that you can mail to Billy's girls!" Then with an added enticement of picking up some take-out dinner, she finally agreed.

We had a fun afternoon, laughing about my purchase of a silly doll for myself, not the kids. I had hesitated to treat myself, but my usually frugal, practical mom said, "Barbara, you work hard for your money. If that's what you want, buy it!"

When we got back to the house, something I had noticed earlier was starting to worry me, and I asked my mom to step under the bright overhead light in the kitchen so I could take a closer look at her. There it was, not only was her face a strange yellow tint but the whites of her eyes were yellow. She was jaundiced! "Okay, Mom, remember what I said before about looking yellow? You are literally turning yellow! Don't panic, just look in the mirror."

When she saw what I saw, I said, "Mommy, remember that gastroenterologist you saw last summer that checked your gallbladder? You need to make an appointment to see him again as soon as possible." We scheduled the appointment that very day.

Quickly, a CT scan was done of her abdomen, followed by a biopsy of a mass on her pancreas. On the very same day that the prospective buyers of my parents' house signed a binder to purchase their home, my mother received a call from the doctor saying he needed to discuss the mass he found on her pancreas and she needed to come to his office the next day for a consultation. That was the first of many sleepless nights for my parents and me. We decided to hold off on calling my brother and sister in Atlanta until we saw the doctor.

After a brief introduction and politely shaking our hands, my mother, father, and I sat, stone-faced and with hearts pounding, opposite the doctor in his tidy but cramped Brooklyn office where he pulled out her file and opened it. I held my mom's hand. I felt like we were pathetic characters in a movie where the audience was holding their breath and some were getting their tissues ready.

"Mrs. Gomes, I have some bad news for you. You have a tumor on your pancreas and it is malignant. You have pancreatic cancer and I'm referring you to an excellent surgeon at Sloan-Kettering Memorial Hospital in Manhattan. He's a wonderful surgeon and has had much success with this kind of surgery. I would refer my own mother to him. I'm going to prescribe some medications today to handle some of the symptoms you're having and for pain. I will try to answer any questions you have but I need you to promise me one thing: This is a difficult type of cancer to treat and we have found that it is important that the patient has and continues to maintain a very positive attitude. You must be willing to undergo whatever treatments your surgeon will recommend and always keep, above all, a positive attitude and faith. Mrs. Gomes, will you promise me that?"

And with tears in her eyes, my mother replied, "Of course, doctor, I'll do whatever it takes. I'm still young [my mother was just sixty-eight years old], and my family needs me. I have to be here for my daughter."

At which point, I immediately turned to face my mom, who was dabbing her eyes with a tissue, and thought to myself, *My mother is a saint. Instead of thinking of herself, she's thinking of her daughter.* So I interjected, "No, Mom, don't do it for me. You have to do it for yourself!"

My mother replied in a rather annoyed way, "Who's talking about you? I'm talking about your sister!"

"Gee, Mom, you don't have to yell at me!" We all started to laugh.

Then my mother said to me, "You have your husband, Frank, to take care of you, and your brother is a man, but your sister is still single!"

Knowing that my mother meant all that in the best possible way, we moved on and, after asking a few questions, left the doctor's office with the surgeon's name and telephone number.

This was the end of October 1996, and the internet was in its infancy at the time. We knew nothing about pancreatic cancer. I remember we looked up the word *pancreas* in the *Encyclopedia Junior* my brother had won for watching a *National Geographic* TV show when we were kids and correctly answering some questions about the show in a contest.

We take for granted some things, like our pancreas, until something goes wrong. None of us had even heard of someone with pancreatic cancer. My dad poured the three of us a stiff drink, and after another good cry, we decided to call my brother and sister with the news.

My father, always the brave and positive thinking one in the family, always a Marine, explained to my brother and sister what the doctor said and that we should all remain positive and wait to see what the surgeon had to say. After all, he was a specialist. My mother reminded us that saying the rosary and lighting candles would also help. She told us all that, no matter what, she wanted to fight and that she was not going to give up hope.

The next day, my mother obtained an appointment with the surgeon for the Monday after Thanksgiving. Apparently, he was a very busy man, which we all took to be a good sign. My sister would be coming up for Thanksgiving to help us try to have a normal holiday. Well, at least we thought so.

Shortly after the bad news, my mother and dad shared the story with my aunts and the rest of the family, hoping to get as much support and prayers as possible. I asked many of my lawyer friends if any of them had ever dealt with pancreatic cancer. A judge in a Brooklyn court, whom I was very friendly with and respected as being very smart, told me her sister had died of pancreatic cancer, that we should get the best surgeon possible and we should hold onto our seats because it was going to be a bumpy ride.

One of my best friends was a nurse who had started her career at Sloan-Kettering Hospital and when I tried to cancel a girls' day of beauty and yoga we had planned, she insisted, after I told her my reason for canceling, that I should not. After we met at the beautiful and peaceful spa and sat to sip a delicious hot coffee, she told me that now I would really need a day like this because my mother was going to need me to be strong and have my "shit together," as we say in Brooklyn. After that, she gave me a big hug. I was really scared now because my buddy the nurse never talks like this; nothing scares her, but I could see that this did.

My sister and I tried to make that Thanksgiving special for my parents, even though we all were nervous about Mom's upcoming appointment with the surgeon. My brother and his wife called from Atlanta and wished her good luck and put the girls on the phone, which always made my mom happy.

Monday morning finally came, and we met with the famous surgeon who unfortunately had no good news for us. He simply stated that my mother's tumor was inoperable. It was on the mesenteric vein and could not be cut. He told us that only 15 percent of pancreatic tumors were able to be surgically removed. He then bluntly stated that my mom had about two to six months to live. The four of us sat there stunned. We staggered out of the office and drove my sister to the airport so she could be back in Atlanta for work the next day. We all cried. My father said this couldn't be; there had to be a surgeon or a doctor somewhere in the tri-state area that could treat my mom and save her life. After all, if my mom, who was starting to suffer a lot of pain, wanted to fight for her life, how could we let her down? We all vowed not to give up and that we would begin an immediate search to find that doctor. We all hugged my sister as she hurried to catch her flight and made a pact to keep the faith and find help for my mother.

With a lot of networking, we eventually found a doctor in Camden, New Jersey, who was doing experimental treatments for pancreatic and liver cancer. He was associated with a famous teaching hospital, which apparently was more open to new treatments. We made an appointment for the week before Christmas. I'll never forget how sad it was to look at Christmas decorations and see people Christmas shopping and celebrating while my heart was breaking. I went to church as often as possible and lit candles for my mom and made every deal with God that I could think of.

Meeting the next doctor was a completely different experience. He explained to us his novel treatment for pancreatic cancer, which was still in its early stages. My mother had to qualify for the program and so he scheduled another test. He soon told us she was accepted and that he was fairly confident he could help her. The three of us almost fell to the ground to kiss his feet. Here was the hope that we desperately sought.

He said that once a patient was told they had an incurable cancer, they were like someone hanging from the edge of a cliff, and he believed that you don't watch them fall but, instead, you must throw them a rope to grab onto. This treatment was to be the rope and would begin in early January. My parents would drive from Brooklyn to Camden every Sunday night so my mother could receive daily treatments Monday through Friday while they slept at a hotel during the week and returned to Brooklyn for the weekend. This routine would continue for the next two to three months. I insisted on accompanying them for the first week, and I stayed with them every weekend in Brooklyn to help them out.

In the meantime, my sister was not feeling well at all. She was having chest pains that everyone blamed on anxiety over my mother. She was only thirty-two years old and in good physical shape. A doctor insisted it was a hiatal hernia that had bothered her in the past. Luckily, a gastroenterologist she saw wanted her cleared by his cardiologist friend before he did an endoscopy. I spoke to my sister every day, and I couldn't believe how all this was quickly escalating.

My sister was single and living alone, although not far from my brother and his family. My husband's mother and sister, also living nearby in Georgia, and my brother and his wife kept tabs on her. My sister called me a day before we were to head off to New Jersey for mom's first treatment to say she was having a heart cath test that the cardiologist had insisted on. I felt I should fly down to help her but she insisted that my parents needed me more. Our dad had gotten a heart valve replaced less than a year before and was not physically up to dealing with all of this going on with our mother alone.

I agreed to stay home, but only if I could, instead, ask my sister-in-law to go with my sister. Thankfully, my sister-in-law immediately and kindly agreed to go with Christina and promised she would call me at the slightest sign of a problem.

The next day, while I was at my office waiting for my father and mother to meet me to head out to Camden together, I received a frantic call from my sister-in-law. "Your sister was rushed from the heart cath lab right into surgery. She has several substantial blockages. You better get down here right away!"

Chapter Twenty-Seven

While my secretary booked me on the next flight to Atlanta, I had one more thing to do before I could race home and throw some things in a bag. My parents were supposed to pick me up in a couple of hours so I could accompany them to New Jersey and be there with them for my mother's first treatment the next day.

I telephoned my dad and tried to calm myself down so as not to upset him any more than he already was about my mother. When he answered, I explained what was happening with Christina and that I was going to fly to Atlanta that evening so I could be there when she woke up from her open heart surgery. I promised I would call him as soon as I arrived with an update on her condition.

Just as I was telling him not to tell Mom what was really going on and to tell her I had to start a trial, at least until Christina was in recovery, my mother was on the line, demanding to know what was going on. Unfortunately, she had picked up the phone extension in her bedroom and caught the tail end of our conversation. I calmly broke the news to her, and she immediately insisted that she was also coming to Atlanta to be there to help Christina. Somehow my father and I convinced her that she needed to go to New Jersey to begin her own treatments since the doctor had told us that time, for her, was of the essence. She only agreed to do so when I promised her that not only was I going to Atlanta but I would stay with my sister the entire time she was in the hospital and also when she got home for recovery. Mom finally consented.

If I didn't have a heart attack that night, I don't think I ever will. I arrived in Atlanta a few hours later and my brother picked me up at the airport and we made it to the hospital just as my sister was getting out of surgery. We spoke to her surgeon, only to learn that she required quadruple bypass surgery, having had several ninety-percent blockages. He had never had a thirty-two-year-old, otherwise rather fit, young woman require this type of heart surgery. Probably because she was a woman, she had been misdiagnosed for the past couple of months as having gastro problems. He suspected her cholesterol issue was probably genetic and advised us both to see cardiologists.

I stayed with her for a week in the hospital and then another two at her home for her initial convalescence. Both she and I knew I needed to get back home to our parents, as our mother's condition was worsening steadily, and Mom was experiencing much pain and difficulty with her experimental treatments. I sadly left my sister in the hands of my brother and other relatives and arrived home on Staten Island on a Sunday morning.

My parents stopped by my house for a quick lunch as they were on their way to Camden for another week of treatments. As soon as I opened the door and saw them, my heart broke. My dad looked worried and exhausted, and my mother looked terrible. She had lost a lot of weight and was having difficulty eating and was in lots of pain. They asked me to go over what had happened to Christina and everything the doctors had said. Then I learned my mother was on some heavy pain medication, and if her condition continued to worsen, they would admit her to the hospital in New Jersey.

Over the next few weeks, whatever could go wrong for my mother did. She was having terrible pain and difficulty eating, refusing to eat despite our efforts to puree her food. Her sisters, one by one, came to visit and begged her to eat to maintain her strength and tempted her with soups and goodies she might like. I heard my mother crying out for her own mother and father in Italian in her bedroom on the weekends when she returned home from her treatments. My mother was always brave and stoic and had never cried over any pain or illness she ever had over the years. She was tough. I knew this was bad.

Around the clock, she was given pain medication. I remember getting in bed with her one afternoon and praying with her and trying to cheer her up. I asked her if there was anyone she wanted me to send for, like her best friend from childhood, Lita, who was also sending over pureed food to help us out. My father was worn out and exhausted from his own recent heart surgery, and worse than that, he was heartbroken. My sister was in another state recuperating from her own heart surgery and enduring postsurgical complications. My brother was working hard to provide for his wife and three young daughters while also trying to help my sister as much as possible.

So when I asked my mother if I could call her best friend to come over, she looked at me with her sad amber eyes and said, "Barbara, you're my best friend." As long as I live, I will never forget my mother saying that to me. That's when I said, fighting back tears, "Mom, there's some things we have to talk about so that I will know how to take care of everything in case you don't make it. We're going to talk about that now because I want you to instruct me so I can do things the way you want them done. And after we discuss this, we will never talk about it again because that is not going to happen." A very tearful and heartbreaking conversation between us ensued.

Soon, she ended up having gallbladder surgery, and a feeding tube was required. She was admitted to the hospital, even though her treatments were completed, to help her regain her strength. As my dad and I spoke with her oncologist about her surgery, terribly upset about the feeding tube, which we thought would discourage my mother even more now, my father suddenly interrupted the doctor and said, "Doctor, tell my daughter about me now."

That hit me like a punch in the stomach! I knew something bad was coming because my father never was afraid to talk about anything and never asked anyone to speak for him. My immediate response was, "What?! I don't think I want you to tell me anything else today!"

The doctor immediately responded, "Barbara, your father also has cancer—prostate cancer—but don't worry, it's a lot easier to treat than what your mother has, and there's no reason why he shouldn't be fine after treatment." I really don't remember anything else he said, because all I wanted was to wake up from this nightmare that hit the Gomes family. Serious illness had struck my mother, sister, and now my father. We called my brother that night to update him on all this bad news, deciding to temporarily spare my sister, who was having a terrible recovery herself.

When my father handed me the phone, I said, "Billy, take care of yourself, please. This is freaking me out, and I'm feeling like there's some kind of curse. I'm not kidding, get some holy water." That night, I called Aunt Jennie to get some advice. I needed to know if prayers were enough. I asked her if we still knew any stregas in the old neighborhood.

My poor mother's condition worsened and the cancer spread to her liver. We brought her home so my dad and I could care for her in the house she loved so much. We got her a hospital bed and took shifts with her. She mostly survived zonked out on morphine for the terrible pain. We called a priest for the last rites.

My sister was finally able to fly in May, and she and Mom spent a few days together. My mom was thrilled and lucid enough to realize her youngest was home with her. My brother came up to visit and help us pack up their house so we could go through with their sale. I persuaded my parents to move in with me and my husband so we could care for Mom together.

The rest of the family came to visit my mother, which would be for the last time. We all, the whole family, were falling apart, realizing the treatments had not worked. But my mom never complained. She mostly suffered in silence. She kept telling us, on the rare occasions she would talk, that she loved us and she would keep fighting.

On June 10, 1997, she spent her sixty-ninth birthday in the hospital, hanging on for dear life. I took off my work suit, put on a hospital gown, and crawled into the hospital bed with her. We took her home to my house by ambulance. My father was finally able to sleep a little. My brother came up to visit again. Mom seemed to be improving somewhat—my brother even got her to laugh. She watched a video of my brother's daughter Annie graduating from kindergarten over and over again. We even set the closing date for my parents' house.

Then suddenly, one morning, she couldn't breathe. The visiting nurse told us to call an ambulance and get her to the hospital. My dad and I were in the ER with her when she was in terrible pain again. My friend, the ER doctor, said that if he administered morphine, it would stop the pain, but it could stop her heart in her condition. My father and I realized we could not see her suffering in terrible pain anymore. It was the hardest decision we ever made. It was seven months after her diagnosis and about a week after her sixty-ninth birthday. My beautiful, strong mother was now dying.

My last conversation with her was in that ER. She reached for my hands as she was panting for air even with an oxygen mask on. Her beautiful, thick, Calabrese, salt-and-pepper hair was recently cut so beautifully by my cousin's wife so Mom would feel more comfortable, and it framed her lovely face that hardly had a wrinkle. She had lost a lot of weight, and she reminded me of how she looked when I was just a little girl. As I leaned in close to her, she kept repeating, "Barbara, I have to fight, I have to fight."

"No, Mommy," I said as calmly as I could, "you don't have to fight anymore. Try to relax and close your eyes. Let the medicine take over. Now it's time to rest."

I choked back my tears. I prayed more prayers.

A few hours later, my mother died. She had fought the good fight.

Chapter Twenty-Eight

The next morning, I had to cancel the closing on my parents' Brooklyn house, and instead, we made funeral arrangements according to my mother and father's wishes. A wake and mass were held in Brooklyn, and my mother was buried in Roswell, Georgia, near where my brother and sister lived.

My father could not stand to remain in Brooklyn without my mother there and wanted to carry out the plans that he and my mother had made to retire to Georgia. He only stayed with me and my husband to have a surgical procedure for his own cancer, insisting he would be well enough to have his radiation treatments down south.

Before he left, my father and I, just the two of us, like we had done for several years when I was a teenager, took a few days for a trip, this time a farewell trip, to New London, the little city where the Aguiars and the Gomes family had settled. Thinking it would probably be our last trip together there, we visited the cemetery and took flowers to the graves of his parents, his grandparents, and his aunts and uncle. We drove by the old neighborhood where Mama had lived and had a last look at her comfortable old house with the railroad tracks behind it, on Maple Avenue. We saw a few of his older Aguiar cousins and hugged and kissed them all good-bye, as they wished my father good health and happiness as he started anew in the South.

Unable to dissuade him from making the move so quickly, he left for Georgia, underwent several weeks of radiation treatment, and found a quaint house in the woods just like the one he and my mother had dreamed about. He was like a man on a mission to renovate the house and settle in.

He enjoyed spending time with my sister, brother, and my brother's sweet wife and three beautiful daughters. He attended Grandparents' Day at his youngest granddaughter's grammar school. He joined the Knights of Columbus in Roswell and the Italian Club (he told me that he was Italian by osmosis) in an effort to make friends. He volunteered to play Santa Claus for the Knights at Christmastime. He took up bird watching, something he had always wanted to do when he was finally a man of leisure, bought a book about birds of the South, and bought himself and all of us bird clocks that chirp a different bird every hour, in an attempt to drive us all crazy, and so we would always think about him. Little by little, all the divorced or widowed older ladies from both my sister's Catholic church and my sister-in-law's Baptist church started leaving a covered dish with their phone number tucked inside since he was a very eligible sixty-eight-year-old handsome bachelor with his own teeth and still driving his new white suburban.

This was about when, after he had settled down and set up his new house the way he and Mom had wanted it, the phone calls started coming hot and heavy. He would call me during my workday, not realizing I was so busy in the middle of the day, and when I would try to rush off the phone, he'd tell me, "Oh, you're at work—geez, when you're retired, every day is Saturday." Most of the time he called for no real reason at all or to ask me how my mother would do something or cook something. He told me once that he started a project of putting all of our old family photos in albums.

"You know what I realized?" he asked me so sadly and with

such regret. "Working six days a week all those years and looking at all the photos of you three kids growing up, I saw how much I missed of you kids and how lucky Mommy was to have so much time with you, Billy, and Dee."

Of course, this caused me to gulp, and tears welled up in my eyes. "We knew you loved us, Dad!"

"I hope so," he replied.

One call that left me speechless, "Hello, Barb, this is Daddy."

"Daddy, it's after midnight," I replied.

"Is it? I didn't notice. I've been keeping crazy hours lately. You know what I realized honey?"

"No, what's that, Dad?"

"No matter how far from Brooklyn I move, no matter how much I fix up my little house here in the woods, no matter what I do, I still miss Mommy."

"I know, Dad," I said, "I really miss her too."

Chapter Twenty-Nine

A t about the end of his first year in Georgia, my father began to get sick. My sister and brother did their best to keep after him, inviting him to dinner or lunch and to get-togethers with their friends. They'd drop in on him to see if he was sleeping properly, eating well, and whether he was smoking again. Unfortunately, we soon realized that the man we thought was so independent and strong was really a mess without our mom to take care of him.

First, it was shingles, and then it was pneumonia. The radiation treatments he had received for his cancer had done a number on his immune system. My husband and I stayed with him in his cozy woodsy house for Christmas, and we all gathered and enjoyed our annual Portuguese breakfast because Dad prepared for us his traditional Madeiran dish, *carne vinagre d'alho.*

I caught him a few times that week falling asleep at the kitchen table after midnight with a cigarette in his hand. I talked to him, trying not to lecture him, about not smoking and going to bed early. As usual, he'd pat my hand or touch my cheek and say something like, "Don't worry about your old man, Barbara," or "You're worried about me? You don't have to worry about me, babe; I am strong like bull!"

After the holidays, his pneumonia returned, about the time he took my sister to the Knights of Columbus St. Valentine's dance. She remembers how sweetly they danced together that night, recalling what a great dancer he was and how he and my mother always danced so perfectly together.

Shortly after that, he was admitted to the hospital, and they found he had meningitis. The radiation treatment he had received for his prostate cancer had completely destroyed his normally robust immune system. The man who was never sick all of his life was starting to crumble before our eyes, and the infection in his body finally attacked the artificial heart valve he needed at sixty-seven years old, so now he also had endocarditis. Emergency surgery was performed on my father to replace the infected valve and to reconstruct his bacteria-covered heart, even while he still had meningitis, in a desperate attempt to save his life.

Just before he was taken to the OR, I made it down from New York and to his bedside. In his fever and confusion, he thought I was my mother and put his warm hand (he, just like my brother, was always warm) on my cheek and said, "Oh, my Annie, you came to see me!"

Eventually, he came to and said something so "Bill Gomes." In an attempt to cheer him up after Mom died, I tried to recruit him to take a trip with me to Madeira, to look for his parents' families, which we had lost touch with over the years. He would always uncharacteristically refuse, claiming he wouldn't find anyone or that he was embarrassed he had not done enough with his life to meet his successful Gomes family. I tried to cajole him, shocked that this ever-confident man would feel that way. It was amazing to see how grief had changed him. Then, as they were wheeling him out for such a risky surgery, of which he was well aware, he said with his big, handsome, toothy smile and a hint of one gold tooth he had somehow acquired, "You know what, Barb? When I get out of this, let's go on that trip to Madeira!" Here was that fun-loving, optimistic father of mine I loved so much!

He survived the surgery, remained on a respirator for about thirty days, and then miraculously came to! He drove us crazy to get him out of there and back home. We explained to him that he needed to have some physical therapy for a few days to walk again, and I made plans to return shortly during the Easter break to help him get situated back home. He had a new lease on life and tolerated our requests just barely.

My brother and sister had visited him in the hospital on Palm Sunday, and while my sister was with him, he began to feel ill. She did her best to pamper him with grooming and complained to the nurse, but suddenly he reached out to her and couldn't breathe. A code blue was immediately called.

So while I was visiting with Aunts Anna, Jennie, and Rosie in Brooklyn since I would be in Atlanta with my father and the rest of my family for Easter, I received a hysterical call from my sister. My father was dead. He survived the battle (the surgery), as they say, but lost the war. One year and nine months after my mother had died at sixty-nine years old, my father had now died at sixty-nine on Palm Sunday, 1999. This, after everything he had gone through, all resulting from treatment for his prostate cancer that was "not as serious as your mother's cancer."

Chapter Thirty

T he time after my father died, and a few years after Frank and I left New York to join our families in Atlanta, is pretty foggy. Initially, I was a woman on a mission. Numb from all the sorrow and struggling to be the head of the family that my parents had expected me to be, I pushed on. Not that I was anything special, just that I was the oldest of our Gomes family and I was an attorney. I had been with my father through all of my mother's funeral plans and the cleaning out of and sale of our beloved house in Brooklyn, and now it was time to do the same with his woodland house in Woodstock, Georgia, or the house of unfulfilled dreams as I have come to think of it.

It was supposed to be a new beginning for both of my parents, who had put off all their dreams of being just a "couple" again, who had worked out all their frustrations of facing old age and then finding themselves again. They had finally reconciled with a meeting of the minds and hearts, a renewal of their love and marriage vows, spiritually and physically, only to end up both in an early grave. What had my parents done to deserve such a tragic ending?

As the final straw, my closest cousin, my other brother as I always thought of him, was terminally ill at just age forty-seven. I heard him sobbing uncontrollably at my father's funeral mass. I knew how much he loved my father, his uncle Bill, his godfather. They had shared a special bond. They were two men with huge hearts who loved to live on the edge, especially when they were young. They both had fathers who were born in Europe, one from Madeira, Portugal, and the other from Bari, Italy, and who were very strict and demanding of their sons. Their fathers had come from the old school of thought that boys should be raised to be "macho" and follow the path in life chosen for them by their fathers, not by the sons.

My father had always been there for my cousin, through thick and thin, and was his emergency phone call, just like my aunts had been for me when I had gotten into a predicament as a teenager and was too afraid to ask my mother for help.

After a couple of family phone calls, I learned that my cousin was very sick and probably not going to make it. Could God punish us anymore? I was about ready to jump off a roof for the first time in my life. I could not take one more loss. I frantically decided my husband and I needed to leave everything behind and start all over again in Georgia, where three of our four siblings and our nephews and nieces were living. I needed a drastic change and tried to run away from all the mourning and death we had been dealt. On my last visit with my dearest cousin, with whom I had shared so many secrets and adolescent rites of passage, he held my hand and kissed me on the forehead from his hospital bed as he impishly smiled at me with his piercing deep black eyes and said, "Bobbie, you and Frankie have to go now, don't waste any time. It sounds like my kind of adventure." Within months, we were gone, and sadly so was my beautiful cousin Dominick on his final adventure.

Leaving New York and moving to Georgia was one of the best decisions we ever made. The weather was better, it was less crowded and stressful, the cost of living was cheaper, and the best part was that we were closer to our immediate family again. When you grow up in a big Italian American family as my husband and I did, there are just certain things that make you happy and make your life complete, especially if you don't have any children of your own as, unfortunately, was the case with us no matter what we tried.

For me, being with my brother and sister again healed my wounded soul. Even though it meant practically starting over professionally for both of us, it was just the challenge we needed in our boring middle age, and fishing for bass on our little pontoon on the lake behind our house was just the transition that we had in mind. Okay, there was no Brooklyn "flava" and you couldn't find good pizza, bagels, or Chinese food, but my brother kept my sister and me laughing with his crazy accents and antics, and that was just what the doctor ordered.

Frank and I would laugh and say, while sipping wine on our little boat, "Not bad for two kids from Brooklyn," as we watched the setting sun, fish biting, turtles coming up for air, and deer prancing across the golf course.

Spending more time with our sisters and brother was restorative, especially enjoying time again with our two lovable nephews, Frank's sister's sons, who had also moved to Georgia from the Northeast, and our three nieces, who were all growing up in leaps and bounds. I felt terrible about leaving Aunt Anna and Jennie back in Brooklyn, but I called them daily and visited a couple of times a year and helped as much as possible remotely from my new home in the South. They would not come to Georgia no matter how much I pleaded, giving me the old "I was born in Brooklyn, and I'm gonna die in Brooklyn" line.

It wasn't all hunky-dory, but it was living again, not just mourning. My sweet sister married her old flame, Tom, from New York, shortly after September 11, 2001. Our family was lucky to have been removed by then from the World Trade Center; both my sister and I had worked at various times in the towers, my brother in the Wall Street area for years. My husband was lucky to have escaped that tragedy, now working in law enforcement in Atlanta and not NYC, and his brother narrowly escaped death as an NYC fireman, having just retired—almost everyone in the firehouse where he had been working in Manhattan was killed. So when my sister and her sweetheart married down here about a month later, it was more than a wedding party. It became a celebration of life.

It was about six years of normalcy until that family curse came back to rear its ugly head. Out of the blue, I had a stroke at work one day, preparing for a trial. Fortunately, my office mates, realizing what was happening, rushed me to the emergency room of nearby Emory University Hospital, where I was told the reason I couldn't see was either because I was having a stroke or I had a brain tumor. Lucky for me, it was a stroke and they caught it just in time. Turns out, I had been born with a hole in my heart and it finally caught up with me in my fifties. Thankfully, it was easily repaired, and although my vision and balance, among other things, remained impaired, I survived. It was a scary close call and I was thankful to be alive. I couldn't help but think that if my father was still around, he would have made a joke that he knew I had a hole in my head, never in my heart.

I thought, *Will this be an early retirement, or will my brain correct itself as the doctors opined hopefully within a year?* I decided to do the best I could with all their suggestions to get my brain back in order and with physical therapy. I'm not a very patient person, and I like to take matters into my own hands, but I was learning the hard way how illness or sickness can teach one humility quickly. I tried to learn acceptance from my much younger sister. She had already been dealt a terrible battle with heart disease beginning in her thirties and learned how to handle her illness with grace and a positive attitude. For good measure, we dug out Mom's collection of "horns" and filled up on holy water, trying to battle these unfortunate events scientifically and spiritually if possible.

Things weren't going too well for my brother either. I mentioned how handsome he was, and in fact, he won a beauty contest for little boys when we were on vacation at Pleasant Acres in the Catskills as kids. I have my parents' slides to prove it. His prize was an ice-cold bottle of soda—it was the sixties!

I suppose that even good looks can sometimes be a problem. In his forties now, he had gone through his second divorce, and the stress hit him hard, financially and emotionally. Anyone who has been divorced can tell you how traumatic it can be, especially when children are involved. This time around, he had three daughters, he and his second wife had a daughter together and his second wife had two from her prior marriage, all of whom he loved like his own. He had gotten into the mortgage business, and being such a personable and vivacious guy, he had been doing really well—that is, until the real-estate bubble started to burst in the US, this being 2007. Like many others, he had overextended himself in real estate, and his mortgages were not able to close. Every time we spoke, he was going a mile a minute, and I could see he was stressed to the max.

In August 2007, he asked me to attend a school orientation for his youngest daughter, Annie, who was transferring as a sophomore from a public high school to a local Catholic high school because he was finally scheduling a real estate closing for that day. I gladly went with Annie, my legal pad in hand, to take notes for Bill about the school's requirements and policies. He came to my house that night feeling so relieved that the deal had finally gone through because he was so far behind the eight ball. I offered him a dish of pasta I had saved from dinner and a glass of red wine to celebrate his good luck at work. As usual, he was making me laugh about his antics in business and stories about his girls, Brooke, Brittany, and Annie. He told me about his headaches as a softball coach for Annie's team and the way the girls drove him crazy, even though you could tell that he loved it. He really enjoyed being a "Mister Mom" in those days, trying to work at his business and share custody of his youngest, the only one still living at home.

Afterward, we were sitting in my sunroom enjoying each other's company as we went through my notes. I can remember that evening like it was yesterday. My handsome brother was sitting by the windows with the setting sun on the lake behind him, wearing his professional-looking work clothes and his favorite boots with his own notepad in his hands. "I mean really, Bill, boots in August in Georgia?" We laughed some more. He was one of the few people I'd allow to sit in my father's old black-leather recliner, which I still swore smelled like my dad's favorite cologne after all those years.

Billy and I had a trait in common, that we loved to write down notes and to-do lists, an old habit that I suspect we picked up from our own days at Catholic school. After our work was done about what he needed for Annie for the new school year, he mopped his forehead with his handkerchief (a trait he and my father always had in common, since they were always warm), and he stood up and said, "Barbrucell, I gotta get going!" He had lots of nicknames for all of us, just like my dad had before him. Our father called Billy "Charlie Brown" and Dee and me "Asmerelda" and "Mezhmanunda." Billy told me when I called him on his cell phone, "Barbara's cell" would always light up on the screen, and so lately he liked to call me "Barbrucell" with a nice Italian accent for emphasis.

I walked him to the front door and out to his car in the driveway and commented that I didn't like the way he was walking. He brushed it off and said he was working out on the treadmill lately and experiencing pain in his legs. Always the "worrier," I asked him if he had gone to see a doctor for a physical lately. What he said in response will haunt me for the rest of my life.

"Come on, Barb, me strong as bull," as he pounded his chest like the Mr. Macho he was. "I'm going to outlive you *and* Dee!" We kissed good-bye and he gave me my favorite brother bear hug, and I watched him drive away.

Within a few short weeks my beautiful (baby) brother was dead, dying of a massive heart attack at forty-nine.

Chapter Thirty-One

I was in shock and so were our family and friends and anyone who knew my brother. If it weren't for alcohol, I would not have made it through the wake and funeral. Nothing had prepared us for this. My brother had dropped his daughter off at her new high school, gone home to get ready for work, and never made it to his office. I received a phone call from his girlfriend to meet them at the hospital, and within an hour, we learned from a doctor that he had been dead on arrival of a massive heart attack. How do we tell his youngest daughter who was still living at home with him and alternately with her mother, my brother's ex-wife? I will never forget that day, the saddest day of our lives.

Since my brother was not married at the time and his daughters were too young, it fell to my sister and me to make all the funeral arrangements. Billy was buried in the same cemetery as our parents and we found a grave for him nearby. As with all funerals, about a week after the burial, you are faced with the reality of all the things that must be done next. Since I'm an attorney and I was still home from the stroke I had suffered about a year before, I handled his affairs as best I could for him and for his youngest daughter, who was still a minor. I can't tell you how many nights I cried myself to sleep, just like the rest of us who loved Billy so much.

Then came the guilt. I should have died, it should have been me. After all, I was the oldest and I just suffered a stroke. No one needed me—my husband and I were childless, and my husband was young enough to take care of himself and to even remarry. I'll probably never get over this guilt.

All I could do was throw myself into straightening out my brother's legal and financial affairs and be there for my youngest niece. I made a promise to my brother then that I would always be there for his girls who loved him like crazy. Of course, my sister and her husband, my husband, their mother, and their grandmother were all there for the girls too, but I was the one who was at home since the stroke cut my legal career short after twenty-five years. The older girls were living out of state, married, and having children of their own. My brother had previously asked me to help Annie with her studies, and I was somewhat familiar with her new school, having gone to the orientation for him and having attended Catholic school for twelve years, just as my sister and brother had done.

I helped Annie as best I could to adapt to the stricter life of Catholic school, how to study for exams, do research, and write her papers. She was always very smart and a good student, she just needed some direction and advice. The poor kid was full of sadness and anxiety over the sudden loss of her beloved dad and was also expected to jump in academically as a sophomore in a much more demanding and structured high school. She gave it her all and we enjoyed our study sessions, and she had lots of support from the faculty and counseling staff at her new school. I was so proud to see how much she enjoyed the challenge and how much she looked forward to getting into the college of her choice.

I got so much more from helping my niece during this time. My niece, my sister, and I worked together, laughed and cried together, always keeping my brother's memory alive. For me, my profession had always been a substitute for the other big hole in my heart that I had from being childless. Once I was unable to work, I was beginning to feel useless. Now I had a new purpose. I thought of myself as a "fill-in dad," trying to be there for my brother—if I in some way could—to give the girls advice and my time if they ever wanted it.

As the weeks became months and months became years, before you know it, the person you thought you could never live without is gone for a long time, and you realize that, as my father loved to tell us, "time marches on." You want time to stop so that, in some sense, you don't feel so far away from your loved one, but life doesn't work that way.

With my niece all grown up, I needed to find new ways to fill my time and try to enjoy retirement with my husband. He and I wanted to travel and try to do all those things people put on their bucket lists and then, like my parents, find that they waited too long to do. We had dreamed of a trip to Italy and Portugal to explore our family roots and, if possible, reconnect with long-lost relatives of either of our families. In both of our cases, without our grandparents or great-aunts and uncles around to correspond with their beloved family back in Europe, we were slowly losing touch with all of them and losing this important connection to our very heritage. It's difficult to do that kind of searching abroad while you're still employed and limited time-wise.

Years before in 1998, we had gone on a trip to Italy, visiting the towns in Bari that my husband's grandparents had come from, and in Rome, we were able to visit Nana's nephew Roberto's family. With Nana and Uncle Gennaro having passed away, we had lost touch with Roberto's family in Rome.

Although we had learned that Roberto had passed away, on a whim, I made a phone call from our Hotel Bernini to his wife and her daughters, Rosetta, Silvana, and Anna, wondering if they would remember me. To our complete joy, we found they were still living in the same home in Rome, and we planned to meet the next day. When the three of them arrived at the hotel, every one of the staff was waiting excitedly with me in the lobby, and we all cried and then laughed as Frank and I had a group hug with my cousins and all of us got stuck in the lobby revolving door. When we finally "unhugged," we went to a café to get reacquainted.

They remembered me as the American hippie cousin who came to visit them back in the seventies. I had kept in touch with them initially, writing a thank-you letter with Nana and writing about my impending marriage to Frank in the late seventies. One of the first things they did when we were seated at the café was to pull out of Rosetta's purse our wedding photo which I had sent them in 1977.

We explained that we had planned this trip for our twentieth wedding anniversary but I was too brokenhearted to take a trip in 1997, the year my mother had died. So here we were with them amazingly in 1998. We laughed and cried and hugged and kissed, talking about Roberto and how he had been so honored for his distinguished work as a carabinieri in their hometown of Rossano, Calabria. We got to meet a friend of theirs who had once been a mayor of Rossano and gave me a souvenir poster of Calabria to take home.

Frank and I spent a couple of glorious days with them, visiting and touring Rome. This time we kept in touch, and the next year my cousin Silvana was sent by her employer, an Italian telecommunications company, to study English at Berlitz in New York City for a week. She stayed with us for a few days while we took her around to meet some of the American family, in particular my aunts Anna and Jennie.

My aunt Anna was especially excited to meet Silvana and proudly showed her a photo of Nana's sister Anna, Silvana's grandmother. Nana had saved that photo, which she took with her on the voyage with her brother Gennaro in 1920. Silvana was given a copy of this beautiful portrait of Anna, Roberto's mother, that same favorite nephew of Nana's. Silvana cried since she had never seen this beautiful portrait of her stately grandmother, whom she never got to meet, and my aunt cried because she was named after her aunt Anna and, finally, was meeting the beautiful granddaughter of the woman for whom she was named. Again, there was a group hug.

On the trip to Italy that Frank and I took in 1998, we had a brief stay in Calabria but only in the city of Paola, an exquisite seaside resort on the Tyrrhenian seacoast of Calabria. At the time, I happened to have a wonderful client from Calabria whose brother managed a hotel in Paola. So, having no family contacts in Calabria at that time, we decided to stay there.

What an amazing resort it was, with an infinity pool overlooking the seacoast which had cliffs reminding me of Malibu. Since I was his brother's attorney, the manager treated us like royalty. He informed us that we were the only Americans who had ever stayed at this resort, which was, at the time, filled with a fun-loving group from nearby Naples.

I remember waking up my first morning there in Paola, throwing open the shutters, and stepping out onto a balcony that floated above a verdant garden of Eden. Was this Nana's Calabria? I knew, of course, that her city of Rossano was farther south and east, bordered by the Ionian Sea. Then, all of a sudden, from out of the blue, into the hotel's garden came walking a line of young, pretty maidens dressed in white uniforms, carrying baskets on their heads, laden with clean hotel linens. That's exactly how Nana had described the way she transported laundry to be washed on the rocks when she was a young girl. My eyes welled up.

"Frank, wake up, honey! We have to find a way to get to my grandparents' towns!" *How hard could it be?* I wondered. *We were already in Calabria!*

We dressed and rushed down to the lobby to catch our manager friend and asked about getting to Rossano or Longobucco, where my mother's parents had come from. He sent for the cook, who turned out to be a very sweet but gnarly old gentleman who was from Longobucco! We received our very complicated directions to Longobucco and headed out early the next morning.

After a couple of morning train rides, we ended up in the big city of Cosenza where we were instructed by the local train master to wait for the one bus that would take us to the mountain village of Longobucco. This was the same trainmaster that I mentioned earlier who thought I was crazy to go to such a small town where there was only cheese and fresh air.

We sat on a bench for at least an hour as schoolchildren and several older women came and went. The women were dressed in their typical black dresses or basic house coats with their heads wrapped in pretty kerchiefs. Several of them interrogated me as to what in the world two American tourists were doing at this dusty, old, local neighborhood bus stop and how many children we had.

By now, quite worried about this last-minute little adventure, once the bus going to Longobucco finally arrived at our stop, I decided to ask the friendly looking bus driver what time the next bus from Longobucco would be returning to this big city of Cosenza so that we could gauge the extent of our quick visit there that afternoon through evening. His response forced me to shriek and hurriedly turn around, pushing my poor husband, standing behind me, back off the bus! The driver's cheerful response had been, *"Domani!"* *Tomorrow!* Since neither of us was prepared to sleep among the sheep or cheese in the fresh air that night, we decided this would have to be the closest we would get to Longobucco on this trip, and it was time to head back to the hotel, hopefully arriving there in time for happy hour.

Chapter Thirty-Two

Eventually, 2012 was upon us, and it was going to be our thirty-fifth wedding anniversary. It just started to feel like it was time to take a special trip to celebrate and mark this milestone. We had finally tried some cruises—first to Hawaii and second to Alaska. Maybe now I was ready to make that trip to Madeira without my father. After my mom died, I had thought he needed something to bring him back to life and take his mind off of losing my mother. After all, he spoke Portuguese and could help by being our translator, but as you may remember, by the time I finally convinced him to go, he became terribly sick and was gone within a month.

After all these years, I was not as brokenhearted about going there without him. We started to plan a river cruise on the mainland of Portugal on the Douro River in the wine country with a stop in Lisbon and side trip to Fatima. The island of Madeira is closer to Morocco than it is to mainland Portugal. Almost as an aside, I planned that we'd first go to Madeira for a few short days to at least see the island where my paternal grandfather Caesar Carlos, "Charlie," was born and where my paternal grandmother Bella's parents were born. In my mind, I was trying not to make a big deal of the part of the trip that was in Madeira since I was going without my dad, and I had no way to find any of my father's family without him.

I vaguely remembered him once showing me a piece of letterhead or some kind of business paper from someone in his family. I decided to look for it in my father's old file of family papers, which I also believed contained his father's passport. This particular storage box was always so heartbreaking to open, containing not only the estate papers of my mother, father, and his parents' estate but also that of my aunts Anna, Jennie, and lastly of my brother, Bill. I felt, I suppose, that some storage boxes were best left unopened so that, eventually, the yellowing, crumbling papers would be gone through and thrown out by someone else, someone who survived me. Why open up old wounds? At least, that was how I felt back then.

I found the right folder and there was the letterhead of a family business established in 1928 in Funchal, the capital of Madeira. Just as I was thinking, *This probably won't help me much in 2012*, I happened to notice a small yellowing envelope addressed to Mr. Gomes. I carefully opened the aging envelope and two small black-and-white photos, one of a man and one of a woman fell out, two people I did not recognize.

The letter was written in Portuguese, on lined paper, and although I could understand a couple of words, I really could not translate it, except to understand that it was written in Madeira and dated September 9, 1953. *Okay*, I thought, *I'll ask my young Brazilian friend to translate it for me since, of course, she speaks Portuguese*. Who knows if this letter would even help me? I thought it must be written to my father since my grandfather Caesar Carlos was gone by 1953, which was, coincidentally, the same year I was born.

In a few days, I received the translation:

Madeira, September 9, 1953

In God, I hope that everyone is doing well in your family, including your mother and everyone else in the family. In the meantime, our family is doing really well by the grace of God.

I wrote a letter a while back to thank you for the beautiful photograph I received from your wedding. But I still have not received a response to the letter I previously sent. Your father's partner was at my house and told me a lot about all of you. I was very delighted to hear about everyone. My desire was to see you here in Madeira, because in seeing you, I would remember my dear brother since God called him. I was also very happy to know that you are a father. I hope that God gives you and your family many blessings.

With this letter, I am sending a photograph of the eldest aunt in Madeira, because I am sixty years old already. Also, I am sending a small gift with a pilgrimage. I am sending the Holy Fatima card that has been blessed.

One more time, I want to wish everyone in your family well, and my prayers will be with your mother so she gets better. Since your father's partner told me that she was sick, I was very sad to hear she was not doing well. I pray that soon all of you can come to Madeira before I die so we can hug. Since you do not speak Portuguese, please ask your father's partner to write a letter to me through you. For today, that is it. I will write again soon.

I miss your uncle Antonio and all the family. Now, let your mom know that I miss her a lot. Please send her my well-wishes, and for you, a very tight hug from your aunt who wishes health and happiness to you and to your wife and kisses to the girl.

Florentina Rodrigues Gomes

I was sobbing almost as soon as I started to read the translation. A wave of emotions swept over me. I realized that this was a letter written to my father after my grandfather Caesar Carlos had passed away from his aunt Florentina, my grandfather's sister. Apparently, she had received a picture from my parents' wedding and a visit, in Madeira, from my grandfather's business partner and good friend from the old country, a gentleman I remembered from my childhood as Mr. Texeira, or Mr. T. as we called him for short.

I identified with her pain immediately when she explained how happy she was to have a visit from him with news about the family even though seeing my father would have been like seeing her dear, recently deceased brother Caesar Carlos. When I read that she was congratulating her nephew on becoming a father and sending a gift of Our Lady of Fatima's photo that was blessed and with prayers for the girl, the tears really poured, because looking at the letter's date, I realized she was referring to me—I was the baby girl since I had been born just a few short months before the letter was written.

I could feel the concern in her words for my grandmother Bella, who you know was very sick herself at the time my grandfather died and that she died when I was just about two. Florentina seemed desperate to see my father and the rest of us in the family so she could give us a hug before she died, and I cried even more, knowing that my father had never made the trip there. All I could think was, *My dear great-aunt Florentina, now that I lost my own dear brother, who was also so young, I know how much that hug would have meant to you. Was your letter to my father meant to be found by me almost sixty years after you wrote it?*

That's when I vowed to go to Madeira and try my damnedest to find someone in our Gomes family to hug, as, I realized, Aunt Florentina herself was certainly no longer alive. I had this crazy feeling that a hug in Madeira could maybe bring some closure and healing to my family, which certainly needed it!

A couple of months before our big trip to Madeira and river

cruise on mainland Portugal was about to happen, I received a call from a friend of mine that a Portuguese restaurant had recently opened near us, and she thought it would be fun for us to enjoy some Portuguese food in anticipation of the big trip. This sounded wonderful to me because, unlike when we lived up north near Ferry Street in Newark or anywhere in New England, I had never found a Portuguese restaurant around Atlanta. I agreed, and by the next weekend, we were there being greeted by a lovely hostess as we entered Emidio's Portuguese Restaurant.

As our friendly hostess, Maria, led us to a table for four in the very charming establishment, I bravely mentioned that I read about this restaurant on their website and asked where in Portugal the owner or chef was from. I nearly fell off my feet as she answered, "My husband and I are from Madeira."

"What?"

"Yes, Madeira Island is a little Portuguese island located in the Atlantic Ocean, south of Portugal."

"Oh my goodness," I replied, "Yes, I know, my father's family are all from Madeira!"

As my husband and friends looked at me with great big smiles, Frank ordered a nice big pitcher of white sangria to celebrate. Maria returned with our wine and, with her beautiful smile, took our order, which included many of my old childhood favorites my own great-grandmother Mama back in New London would make: *Caldo Verdi* soup and *bacalhao* croquettes.

Shortly after the main course was served, her husband, Joe, the chef, came to the table to welcome us, asked if everything was satisfactory, and said he wanted to meet the American lady whose family was from Madeira. He, too, had a brilliant, friendly smile and asked me, "Where in Madeira is your family from?"

I proceeded to explain that my father's father died before I was born, his mother when I was about two, and that I grew up in Brooklyn, not in New London where the rest of my father's family lived. I further explained that, sadly, we had lost touch with the family in Madeira about sixty years ago. Luckily, I remembered that my grandfather's passport, which I had found in that storage bin, stated he was from Monte, Madeira.

Joe recognized the name of the town and asked if I had ever been to Madeira, to which I replied, "You're not going to believe this, but my husband and I are going for a few days in September."

Then Joe replied, "We are going to help you find your family!" He gave me his number and asked me to call him a couple of weeks before we left for our trip.

Chapter Thirty-Three

W hat I am about to tell you will sound like the makings of a movie or a television episode, but I swear on my father and mother every word is true.

Frank and I were sitting aboard a flight from Lisbon to Madeira when I looked out my window and spotted an Atlantic island that was covered with thousands of twinkling lights. I was trying to take it all in and remembered that in all the tour books, Madeira was called "the Pearl of the Atlantic."

The plan was to hail a taxi to our hotel, check in, have some cocktails, and settle in. In the morning, I was to call Joe's sister Luz and set a time to meet both Luz and their cousin Olivia for drinks that Sunday afternoon on the patio of a restaurant in Funchal, where Joe had worked as a young man and was still friends with the proprietor. When I asked him how in the world they would be able to help me find my family, he calmly and laughingly responded, "No worries, my sister speaks English very well, and my cousin and her husband, Rui, know everyone in Madeira—he works for the government."

Happily, the phone call went smoothly; indeed, his sister spoke English very well, as I had explained many times that I knew very little Portuguese, mostly bad words my father thought was funny to teach a little girl and a nursery rhyme I remember my grandmother Bella and my great-grandmother teaching me. We were to meet later that afternoon, so my husband and I decided to begin our sightseeing in the city of Funchal. I know I'm prejudiced, but everything I saw that day was beautiful. It was a magical place with a subtropical climate in the coastal areas like Funchal and a much cooler climate in the mountains, reachable by either cable cars or very winding, trepidatious roads that had been cut right into the mountains over the years.

Madeira was an uninhabited island discovered by the Portuguese in 1419 by a navigator named Zarco, and it was named Madeira, or "the Woods," because of the dense amount of forest land on the island. A unique irrigation system was built by the inhabitants centuries before and called *"levadoes"* which brought all the rain and snow down from the mountains, where the sheep and goat herders lived, providing much-needed irrigation to the rest of the island for orchards. Most of what you see there is filled with lush and lavish tropical vegetation of cacti, orchids, bougainvillea, banana plants, and birds of Paradise.

We met Luz, Olivia, and Rui, and we immediately hit it off, joking and drinking until Olivia announced she would meet us later for dinner, after work. Much like the rest of Europe, dinner was at about nine o'clock.

We settled down and got to business as I showed Luz and Rui my few documents, my grandfather's passport, the Gomes family-business letterhead (which I thought would be the most helpful with its address), and the letter from our great-aunt Florentina. Rui was our navigator and suggested that since it was Sunday, any business would be closed, so we should take a drive in his car to the neighborhood from which Florentina's letter was written. He explained that although the envelope did not contain a home address, it contained the name and location of the sender's post office.

Off the four of us went for a crazy, winding drive to a very rural-looking neighborhood not far from Funchal, with lots of little houses made of stucco and roofs tiled in orange and red. Luz explained that Rui believed this would be the neighborhood from which that 1953 letter was postmarked. As he drove quickly, often changing gears according to the rolling terrain, he suddenly stopped the car short and pointed to a little building up on a hill. Luz explained that it was a kind of local sports bar or soccer club, which is always the center of attraction and filled with locals from every town. Rui and Frank climbed up the steep driveway while Luz and I remained with the car. In about five minutes, which seemed like forever, Frank came out with Rui and about nine or ten men, all patrons of the bar. Frank motioned to me to come up. Everyone was smiling as Frank explained they wanted to help the Portuguese American lady find her family and needed to see my letter.

I handed them the copy I had made, and they all huddled around reading and passing the letter among themselves while a couple of them who spoke English introduced themselves. They seemed like a friendly crew, if not slightly inebriated, who were genuinely interested in helping me. Those few explained they had learned English in school or while working in Great Britain.

Within a few minutes, the consensus was this: no one knew a Florentina Rodrigues Gomes, but there were two very old people (in their eighties) still living in the neighborhood who might remember her. As a group, we walked a bit to a slightly battered house of an elderly lady who luckily was at home but who answered her doorbell by yelling out of her second-floor balcony in Portuguese. I was told that she was saying we should all go away and threatening to harm us if we did not.

A few of the fellows laughed, explaining that the poor woman was slightly off and suffering from Alzheimer's and truly meant no harm to us. Disappointed, I said to the group let's try the next neighbor, a gentleman they thought could help, and we walked to a pretty little house with an exotic flower garden and lovely front deck. This stop looked a little more promising.

In order to ring the doorbell, one yanked on an actual rope

that caused a little bell at the end to clamor and tinkle. For all its charm, the second home failed to yield any information because, as much as we rang the quaint doorbell, no one responded to all of us waiting outside in front of the house.

Once again, as a group, we walked away and headed back to the sports club. Just as they all were trying to console and cheer me up, my always-alert husband pointed up to a close-by hill and said, "I wonder if he could be in that group up there walking down the hill?" Immediately, our lively group of helpers excitedly said, "Oh yes, of course, those are the people coming down the mountain after the Sunday evening mass!"

Sure enough, within about ten minutes, among a small group of the faithful, we spotted a very nicely dressed, tall, thin, silver-haired gentleman, whom they called Mr. Texeira (ironically the same name as my grandfather Caesar's business partner). As they motioned and called to him to join us, I noticed that this handsome gentleman in his neat gray suit and with his beaming smile appeared to be in his eighties. In Portuguese, my new band of friends explained to him that I was looking for my family and I asked him if he would look at my letter.

With that, he excused himself so that he could go home and get his reading glasses. Nervously, I waited for his return as we all stood around anxiously smiling. Rui and Luz encouraged me that, hopefully, I would get some information. Finally, Mr. Texeira returned, dressed in a stylish jogging suit, with his eyeglasses.

As he read my letter, he began to cry, and when the small photos of my great-aunt and uncle fell out of the envelope, he stopped crying enough to tell me and my new friends, who were all huddled around, that he knew Florentina very well and that sadly she had passed away a long time ago.

I had assumed that much already since this was 2012 and she was sixty when she wrote her letter in 1953. He then pointed to where her house had once stood, which was very close to where we were all standing, and was now just a lovely field of banana trees. Now I was crying, thinking that amazingly I had come so close to Florentina but just too many decades late. Then I noticed that my sweet new friend Mr. Texeira started smiling and, while hugging me, said that he had some good news to give me also. As I waited hopefully, he told the men, my translators, that not only had he known Florentina and her husband, but that his very own sister had married my cousin! With that, I almost fainted right there and then! Of all the people on Madeira Island, I had bumped into an eighty-year-old man who was related through marriage to my family!

With this unbelievable revelation, one of my new friends asked him if he could call his sister and tell her I was here and would like to meet my family and handed him their cell phone. He took the phone and called, but unfortunately, there was no answer. He tried again with the same result. He offered to call again tomorrow and try to make arrangements, and Luz agreed to call him and find out what happened so she could convey the message to me. This seemed like a wonderful plan to me so I conferred with my husband to discuss a way to thank all these very kind and helpful Madeirans, and Frank said, "My wife and I would like to invite all of you back to the sports club for a drink!"

With that, I walked with all my new friends up the hill to the bar, where we feasted on beer, Madeiran wine, and, of course, delicious Portuguese sausage, *linguisa*. Eventually, we left with a hug and good-luck wishes from one and all, especially my new connection, Mr. Texeira.

I couldn't believe it myself as I repeated to Olivia when we met her for dinner what had transpired that evening. She, Rui, and Luz hugged us good-night at our hotel and Luz promised to call me tomorrow as soon as she heard from Mr. Texeira. I don't know how I slept at all that night!

Chapter Thirty-Four

F rank and I decided to go on with our sightseeing plans the next morning, not knowing if we would ever hear from my family at all. We went to Monte by riding a cable car from Funchal and saw their beautiful and exotic tropical gardens and a lovely view of this magical island and its gorgeous harbor, where a couple of cruise ships were docked. Then we paid a visit, or what I felt was rather made a pilgrimage, to the Church of Our Lady of the Mount built in the eighteenth century, which sits at the top of a mountain overlooking the city of Funchal and the sea. I just felt that by going to the church in Monte, I could be in a place certainly where my grandfather had visited. I had read that on August 15, the feast of the Assumption of the Virgin Mary, pilgrims, on their knees, climbed up the seventy-four steps leading up to the beautiful church.

I walked up those steps and entered the beautiful church where I said some prayers. I decided to light three candles, one for my mother, one for my father, and a third for my brother, asking for their intercession and hoping they would help me now that I had finally made it to Madeira and was on a search.

I stepped outside, looking for Frank, who was watching the famous Portuguese fellows who race down the mountainside on toboggans filled with tourists from Monte back to Funchal. I strolled over to a beautiful lookout site to get a better view of the sun, which was starting to set, when I noticed three sweet dogs, golden retrievers, following me, and I started to laugh because their sizes reminded me of a father, mother, and baby dog, and I had this strange feeling that it was my own parents and brother sending me a sign. I know that sounds crazy.

With that, we hopped on a cable car to head back to our hotel and see if any messages awaited us. But there was nothing at the front desk. Frank and I had already decided: no matter what happened, we would go out to dinner with Luz, Olivia, and Rui and celebrate with them since they had helped us so much and were already treating us like family. The telephone in our room was blinking that a voicemail had been left. It was Luz asking me to call her at home when I heard her message. The conversation went like this:

"Hello?"

"Hello, Luz, this is Barbara."

"Hello, my friend, did you enjoy your day in Madeira?"

"Yes, Luz, it was wonderful. I'm so happy, but did you speak to Mr. Texeira?"

"Oh, yes, I did."

"And?" I asked so anxiously. "Can I meet my family?"

"No, I'm sorry, you cannot."

"Oh no . . . well, that's okay, Luz, but Frank and I want to at least take you three out for dinner tonight and hear some Fado singers because you are like my family in Madeira now. I appreciate how hard you guys tried to help me!" Fado is a style of singing, a musical genre that originated in Portugal and is characterized by mournful tunes and lyrics and infused with a sentiment of resignation, fate, and melancholia, which I thought was certainly appropriate for me tonight.

Luz responded, "Okay, that sounds like fun, but your family can see you tomorrow!"

Again, I almost fainted!

The next day, Olivia, Rui, and Luz picked us up from our

hotel in the late afternoon. I was so anxious and excited that I could hardly wait. Again, I lit candles praying for success in finding my family, this time in Se Catedral do Funchal, dedicated to Our Lady of the Assumption, whom I remembered to be my grandmother Bella's favorite saint. It is a beautiful church built in the 1490s in a simple Gothic style and Moorish influences with three naves. It was dedicated as a cathedral in 1517, when Funchal was the largest diocese in the world since it covered all territories discovered by the Portuguese, from Brazil to Japan. No wonder my great-grandfather Adelino Aguiar was insulted when arriving in Lisbon en route to America, and he was told by the Lisbon parish priest to turn around and attend mass in the lower level with the rest of the peasants!

I asked my friends' advice as to what gifts I could bring on this visit, and we selected a box of chocolates and bouquet of flowers. I was equipped with old passports and a couple of family photos and, of course, my great-aunt Florentina's letter. We drove to a beautiful house located in the hills of Funchal that was surrounded by a wall. I could barely speak, a nervous wreck, only learning that someone was willing to meet me but not knowing who it would be.

We rang a bell at the gate as two women came to meet us—a beautiful younger woman, perhaps in her forties, and a lovely woman with silver hair, in her eighties. They were all smiles, and very polite, as they pulled open the gate and nodded hello as I handed them the small gifts I had brought with me.

It was Olivia, Rui, Luz, Frank, and me, and Luz translated a few niceties uttered since the women both only spoke Portuguese. As we entered the beautiful house, I was greeted by a very pretty teenage girl, who was named Marta, but everyone, I learned later, called her Nina. We were invited to sit in their charming living room while Nina went to get her grandfather. She returned, followed slowly by a well-groomed and rather serious-looking older man, also looking to be in his eighties, who was wearing a beige designer-style racer jacket, which immediately relaxed me, as I remembered that my brother loved his very own similar jacket back when we were younger in the eighties.

Once the man sat down comfortably in a cushioned chair next to me, I began my "spiel" that I had been rehearsing all day. I briefly thanked him for meeting us like this, so out of the blue and on such short notice as we were leaving for Lisbon and the river cruise of Portugal in two days. I learned that the gentleman who helped us back in Florentina's neighborhood was the brother of his wife, Teresa, who was still smiling sweetly at me. I explained that I was the daughter of William Charles Gomes, the only child of Caesar Carlos Gomes, who came from Madeira to the US, and of Bella Aguiar Gomes, who was born in America, a daughter of Adelino Aguiar and Maria Clara Aguiar, who also came to America from Madeira. I further explained that all of these relatives were already gone, including my own parents and younger brother and that I had traveled here with my husband and these friends were helping me. He seemed a little sad to hear so many of my family had passed away.

I don't know why, but I think when Nina asked how or when my grandparents had died, I said my grandfather Caesar was about fifty when he fell to cancer, and as I spoke these simple words in English, this gentleman whom I learned to be Jose Damasio Gomes said at the same time in Portuguese, interpreted by Nina as I stated the words in English, "And my grandmother Bella died of stomach cancer." I immediately started crying and so did he since we both knew right then that we were family.

Poor little Nina, our interpreter, started to cry too, and when I looked around the room, I saw my husband and my three new friends along with Teresa and their daughter Alexandra all crying! It was the moment of truth, the moment of recognition and acceptance!

Almost immediately, Damasio raised his hand and, with a beautiful smile, reminding me of my father's smile, told his daughter something like, "What are you waiting for, go get the good wine!" They had already offered us aperitifs but now this was turning into a celebration and felt like a scene from a movie! Nina said her grandfather was very pleased to finally meet me, and we both stood up and gave each other a very big and long overdue hug!

I held my great-aunt's letter in my hand and wanted to kiss it up to heaven and say, "This one's for you, my dear aunt!"

Damasio next called out to Alexandra, "What are you waiting for? Call your brother," as the wine and glasses were passed around! Everyone was laughing and hugging as we all now could relax and be jolly!

I remember Nina looking at my face and telling me, "I knew you were family because you have the same nose as my grandfather!" I laughed as I observed that, under his stylish eyeglasses, he indeed had the same hooked nose I was born with and had despised all my life—until this day! Just then, a handsome young man walked in the front door, dressed nicely in a business suit, bearing a big welcoming smile, and I almost died right there and then because he looked so much like my very own brother Billy!

He came to sit next to me and Damasio and introduced himself to me in English as Joao, the son of Teresa and Damasio, brother of Alexandra. I could see that he was a fun guy and so happy to meet us. We filled him in quickly on how we had found his parents two days before and introduced him to Frank and our friends. He translated for his father that Damasio's father and my grandfather Caesar were brothers. So my grandfather was this elderly gentleman's uncle.

Soon, I was shocked to learn that Damasio had even met my grandfather. He recalled that my grandfather had gone back to Madeira around 1950 when Damasio was nineteen years old and that he was given the honor to drive my grandfather all around Madeira to visit their family and his friends. I vaguely remembered hearing that my grandfather had taken this trip home once just before he died and that my grandmother Bella was too sick to accompany him.

He then told me and Joao that my grandfather quickly became his favorite uncle because he was so much fun and so generous and that he enjoyed helping his uncle organize parties everywhere they visited, complete with food and wine and musicians.

I vowed that once I returned home, I would dig out the old Gomes family album to look for photos that had been left to my father and eventually to me. Damasio asked when we were leaving Madeira, and when he learned we were leaving in two days, he announced that he was taking all of us out to dinner tonight to celebrate. Soon, Alexandra's husband Paolo arrived home to join the party, and we learned that their son Joao Francisco was away in Lisbon, studying in medical school.

Bear in mind, it was about 8:30 p.m. and I was already feeling drunk from all of our toasts and not having eaten most of the day from nerves. I was also drunk with happiness, the kind I had not felt in a long time, maybe since my brother had died. We were given a tour of their beautiful home, which included a large terrace with an amazing view of the city of Funchal and the seacoast below with thousands of twinkling lights in the now-dark surroundings.

I learned that my cousin Joao was an attorney like me, and we laughed, joking that we must be related since the Gomeses as attorneys were troublemakers on both sides of the Atlantic. I could not get over how much he and my brother looked alike in facial features, coloring, height, weight, and age. When I asked him if he was married and he replied, "Sometimes." I knew then he was also a funny guy, just like Billy.

They brought out some family photos of Damasio's father, who was my grandfather Charlie's brother, and he was another handsome Gomes gentleman. Suddenly, I recognized a photo of a beautiful, dark-eyed, olive-skinned nun dressed in a white habit. Could that be the same nun whose photo was displayed in our house growing up as kids? I had been told she was Grandfather Caesar's sister Olinda and that she was a missionary nun. I found out from my cousin Joao that when she was young and fell in love, her parents, my paternal great-grandparents were displeased with the young man with whom she became enamored. As it was done in the old country, the poor young girl was sent to a convent with a broken heart.

The story was that she eventually found peace and happiness as a missionary nun, and she was sent to Mozambique, where she served the church as a teacher of young children. I was curious about her fate, so struck by the life of a young woman in the early 1900s in Portugal, and was happy to hear she was sent back to Madeira eventually, where she lived the last twenty years of her life. In my fantasy happy ending, I imagine that Great-Aunt Olinda found her star-crossed lover upon her return to beautiful Madeira and lived those remaining years of her life with him.

We all went to dinner at a wonderful local restaurant, where we were treated like kings and feasted as such. Delicious Madeira wine was poured, and we ate *espetada*, which is deliciously grilled beef, pork, and lamb that's served on long skewers, then hung from the ceiling so that their flavorful juices run down onto tasty Portuguese bread. I have always been a devout meat eater, so much so that when I was a kid, my mom nicknamed me "Rover." Between that and the wine, I'm sure I was acting ridiculously giddy as we continued to catch up on the sixty or so years of family stories since the Gomes family in America had lost touch with our beautiful Gomes family in Madeira.

We ate, laughed, and drank until we could do no more. I swore I would return in a year or two with the remaining Gomeses in my little family—my sister, Christina, and her husband, Tom, and my brother's daughter Annie—so that they could all meet. We all exchanged numbers and addresses and hugged until we could hug no more. I learned that there was a street in Madeira named for my great-uncle, and beaming with pride, I knew I had to return. Our friend Rui had planned to take Frank, Luz, and me on a driving tour the next (and our last) day to see as much of the island as possible before we left.

We needed to visit Câmara de Lobos, the Valley of the Nuns, Santander with the teepee houses, ride to the top of the island at Pico de Arriero for the walk in the clouds, and drink some *poncha* to warm ourselves in the cool mountains of Madeira, where the goats and sheep roamed the countryside.

Joao said his father wanted to give a parting gift to us, and he would drop off a package for us at the hotel. We said good night—not good-bye—and I barely slept a wink that night.

The next day was very exciting as Rui covered as much territory as possible by car in a day. We dined with him and the girls again that night, marveling at how we had succeeded in finding my family. I felt so sad to say good night to them at our hotel yet so thankful for what they had done. We hugged and kissed, and when Frank and I made our way back to the lobby, we found that Joao had left several bottles of wine for us that his father had made himself.

As soon as I could unpack and meet my sister, her husband, and our niece to tell them about the miracle that had occurred in Madeira, we began to make plans for two years later, for all of us to visit them in Madeira again. We kept in touch with each other by snail mail and social media. We sent small gifts across the Atlantic, back and forth. I dug out that old photo album belonging to Bella, and sure enough, at the end of the album, there were several pages filled with photos of my grandfather on a trip to some tropical location that, as a child, I had just never realized was actually Madeira.

Immediately, I spotted him: a handsome and much younger Damasio, dressed in white slacks and a white dress shirt in a couple of pictures with my grandfather, who had the same big smile my dad always had and the same big smile I like to think I have too. I sent copies to my cousin Alexandra who confirmed that yes, indeed, her dear father assured that was truly him as a young man.

She confided in me that her father, who had been feeling somewhat depressed about no longer actively working in his own business and down about the illnesses his advanced age had brought, was feeling so much livelier lately and excited we had met. She told me he was so looking forward to our return.

And return we did, two years later. My sister, her husband, Tom, Annie, and I were welcomed again with open arms and, this time, taken to where my grandfather had been raised and the street named after our great-uncle. Alexandra explained that her father had taken great interest in our arrival and there would be a little party that he planned. We even met another daughter of Damasio and Teresa, Dalila, and her family.

Nina was growing into a young woman, and she was about to enter medical school in Lisbon, following in her older brother's footsteps. Again, we talked and laughed, hugged and kissed, and danced at the party Damasio had thrown for us. Just like all good things, our time together was over too soon.

We heard from our cousins a couple of months later that our dearest Damasio, the head of our Gomes family, was very ill. We were all devastated when, merely three months after our second trip, tragically he passed away. For his wife, Teresa, and all of his children and grandchildren, it was terribly sad; he was their beloved patriarch. We all cried. Our first direct connection to our grandfather that we actually had since our father had died fifteen years ago was now gone too.

My husband consoled me, saying I should be thankful I had finally made it to Madeira while both Mr. Texeira and my cousin Damasio, brothers-in-law, both in their eighties, were still alive. After all, it was because of them that we were able to discover my family, tracing the connection from my great-aunt Florentina to Teresa and Jose Damasio Gomes.

He was right—that alone had been a miracle.

Chapter Thirty-Five

I t wasn't very long after my first trip to Madeira in 2012 that I started thinking about Nana, my maternal grandmother Christina, who inspired me many years ago to write this book.

When annoyed by my pestering her with so many questions, she would ask me, "Why, Bobbinella, are you asking me all these things? Are you gonna write a book?" Of course, I swore that I would someday, just to have her answer me and satisfy my curiosity.

But something was still missing. How could I write that book for Nana when something so very important was still left undone? I had been to Italy a few times, as a young college student and then with my husband. I had met some of Nana's family, her dear nephew Roberto, his wife, and his daughters, but I never made it to Longobucco, Calabria, where my maternal grandfather, Dominick, was from (even though we had made a valiant attempt), or to Rossano, Calabria, where Nana was born. Perhaps my little miracle in Madeira had given me false hope, but in 2013, with the help of some of my American LeFosse (Nana's family) cousins, I believed I would be able to locate a family member living in Calabria, in either Longobucco or Rossano.

We were going on a cruise to Greece with friends later in 2013, and our ship was sailing from Venice, so we would be in Italy anyway. By that year, with social media groups all the rage, lots of us LeFosse cousins from Brooklyn had happily reconnected, including descendants of both Nana's sister Victoria and her brother Gennaro.

I asked one granddaughter of Uncle Gennaro if any of them had any contacts with family in Calabria. She referred me to another granddaughter of Uncle Gennaro, whose father had been contacted by a cousin in Rome, but different cousins than those I knew. She told me they had all met on a trip to Rossano, Calabria, many years ago. She sent me a photo of the house where Nana, her sister Victoria, and her brother Gennaro had grown up, along with their other LeFosse siblings. Immediately, I knew I had to go there.

I contacted Jean Pierre in Rome, and he suggested we start a social media group of LeFosse cousins. He would invite the Italian cousins he knew, and we could invite the Italian American cousins we knew. Eventually, our family group began to grow, and I became friends with a few cousins who were descendants of Nana's brother Antonio and her brother Isidoro, some living in Rossano, some in Rome, and one living in Milan. Little by little, we all became quite close and one of the American cousins valiantly started to prepare a family tree for the group.

I will tell you the story about this trip to Italy in reverse order, saving the best for last. We met one of my very dear Italian cousins, also named Vittoria—probably after Nana's older sister— one day in Venice while on the cruise. She and her husband had traveled from Milan to Venice by train to meet us and spend one glorious day together. We had been pen pals on social media for quite a while and were so excited to finally meet in person. There was lots of hugging and kissing (we *are* Italian), laughing, and tears that day as they took us on a special tour of one of my favorite cities in Italy. It was difficult to say good-bye that evening, but we took lots of photos and I promised I would come back again to visit her. (Fast forward a couple of years and we did meet up again, this time in Genoa, with her daughter and son also sharing our unforgettable time together.)

On the way to our cruise that year, we also spent a few days in Rome with four of our close friends from the States who were cruising with us. I had learned from the cousin in Rome that he owned a hotel close to the Trevi Fountain, so we all stayed there a few days before taking a train to Venice to board the cruise.

My cousin Jean Pierre and his wife were such wonderful hosts to all of us; I felt like I had known them all my life. He was originally from Rossano but had moved as a young man to Rome to start his hotel business and raise his family. Amazingly, I was also able to contact Silvana, Anna, and their mom, who were still living in Rome. We all met for drinks one night, and I was thrilled to introduce these Italian cousins, all originally from Rossano, to each other. It was an enchanting night, to meet one cousin for the first time and hear about his life and business in Rome and to catch up once again with my girl cousins, the wife and daughters of Roberto, whom I had first met as a young girl in 1974. Frank and I spent a full day with the ladies, having a delicious lunch with them and spending a cozy, sweet afternoon at Silvana's home near the British embassy.

I have always felt as if these girls were more like sisters to me, just like my American cousins I grew up with back in Brooklyn. I know I must be blessed because I have always felt like my favorite times in life were spent with my family. I believe it was the way we grew up. Who knew all those days of pestering Nana about her life growing up in Italy would lead me to all these adventures in Italy, beginning with her letter of introduction to Roberto in Rome in 1974? Who knew that a yellowing old letter from my great-aunt Florentina to my father would lead me to the family we had lost in Madeira, Portugal?

The night before we left Rome, all of the cousins there feasted like royalty, thanks to the graciousness of our hosts, Jean Pierre and his wife, at the fabulous restaurant of his good friend. I shared my plan to write this book with them and dedicate it to my brave and loving Nana. Once again, we all bid "Arrivederci" to each other, or "Until we meet again!"

Going back to when we first arrived in Italy for the cruise of 2013, before going on to meet the others in Rome and then Venice, we first landed in Lamezia Terme, Calabria. When I discussed with the cousins I met in our social media group, who were the only ones I could find at the time living in Rossano, they invited Frank and me to be their guests and to show us around Rossano. Cousins Maria and Giuseppe were so gracious to be our hosts and welcomed us into their home so wholeheartedly—Frank and I will be forever grateful. We met their son and daughters, Pietro, Maria Grazia, Rosellina, and Giovanna; and many other members of their beautiful, happy family.

Maria and Giuseppe had arranged an itinerary for the few days we visited and somehow managed to fit everything in that I was hoping to see. We feasted, drank, and laughed. Maria is an excellent cook, and Giuseppe is an amazing farmer in addition to his main employment. They shared with us their plates of pasta, sauces, wines, and desserts—all homemade. We visited the beautiful seacoast that Rossano is bordered by and its Cathedral di Maria Santissima Achiropita, famous for housing the Codex Purpureus Rossanensis or the Greek Gospels. They arranged a few other wonderful surprises, for which I will be eternally grateful.

They took us first to the carabinieri station, where Roberto had begun his service as a young man in the Italian military police. Silvana had told me years ago that there had been a ceremony and plaque installed at the headquarters honoring Nana's favorite nephew for his heroic accomplishments, and we all proudly admired it while posing for photos there in Rossano.

Later on, they took me to Old Town Rossano, where I was able to stand right in front of the house where Nana and all her brothers and sisters had grown up. It had changed since a Brooklyn cousin had taken photographs but not too drastically. It was inspiring to me to see Nana's humble beginnings and realize how far she had traveled to leave her mother and siblings, to venture to America at twenty-one, the same age I was on my very first visit to Italy.

My dear cousins also drove us on a three-hour ride up into the mountains to the alpine town of Longobucco, where my grandfather Dominick and his brother Frank were from. It had taken us a long time and many years to get there, but we finally made it. One of the things we did there, upon arriving, was visit the gorgeous church in the center of Longobucco, named Chiesa di San Domenico. There it was, all the way in the front near the main altar, a beautiful statue erected to honor Saint Dominic, who turned out to be the patron saint of Longobucco. I started to cry because now I finally realized that my grandfather was not only named like the town, Longobucco, but that his first name was after its patron saint, Dominic. I never knew that before.

Just when I thought no more dreams of mine could be fulfilled, Giuseppe and one of his daughters, who had done some research work for the family tree that our American cousin was preparing, told me there was just enough time to make a visit to the cemetery in the countryside, where most of our Italian ancestors were buried. We purchased some pretty flowers upon our arrival, and after visiting several gravesites of Nana's brothers and sisters, nieces and nephews, they took me to the grave of the one that meant the most to me.

Italian gravestones are different than most I had seen before in that almost all have a photograph of the dearly departed right on the stone. As the three of us walked around the very old section of the cemetery, my dear cousins walked me over to a very tall monument, and I saw upon it a portrait I knew since I was a little girl! There was the portrait of Nana's mother, Rosaria Sapia LeFosse, my very own Italian great-grandmother. Here was the mother my own Nana had longed and cried so much for, whom she had never seen again since she and her older brother Gennaro had left on their voyage to look for their new home in America.

I placed beautiful roses upon the grave of Nana's beloved mother and I cried again. Although they started as tears of mourning for my grandmother and great-grandmother, my tears transformed into tears of gratitude, for it was Nana's own stories of love and longing that had led me on my own journey of a lifetime, of travel and of writing this family book of mine, as simple and yet as miraculous as it is to me.

Addendum

T his book took me too many years to write because I needed time for its chapters to unfold. I'm the same age now that my parents were when they died and a lot older and wiser than I was fifteen years ago when my writing began. I realized that my story needed to be about more than my nuclear family and that I needed more time to understand my family's beginnings. I'm a great-aunt myself now, and I adore all of my eight nieces and nephews and nine great-nieces and great-nephews, perhaps because they are all the children I never had.

Ironically, it was only my brother, Billy, who had children and grandchildren—my sister and I unable to do so—and he left this beautiful life too soon, and before both of us, his sisters. Joyfully, I must report that our family has now two more family members, named after my own dear brother whom I miss to this very day. One is named Jude William, and one is named William Lewis. I know that my brother is getting as much of a kick as we do out of all of these beautiful children and grandchildren of his, especially when they entertain us with their silliness and antics, just like my brother was famous for, or like when little Billy walks down my staircase after spending the night and calls down to me, "Aunt Baba, good morning. *Ciao, Bella!*"

About the Author

B arbara Gomes Serafino is a retired trial attorney living in the Atlanta suburbs who will always consider herself a "Brooklyn girl." Raised to be proud of her Italian and Portuguese heritage, family has been her greatest joy. In addition to writing and painting, she enjoys amateur astronomy, paranormal radio, and traveling with her husband and friends.

She is pictured above in approximately 1985, as an Assistant District Attorney in Kings County, Brooklyn, New York.

CPSIA information can be obtained
at www.ICGtesting.com
Printed in the USA
BVHW041927160623
666068BV00003B/51